WINDOWS ON WESTMINSTER

DAVID W. HALL

A look at the men, the
work and the
enduring results of the
Westminster Assembly
(1643-1648)

GREAT COMMISSION PUBLICATIONS
7001 PEACHTREE INDUSTRIAL BLVD., SUITE 120, NORCROSS, GA 30092-3652

ISBN 0-934688-79-6

Printed in USA

Published by Great Commission Publications
7001 Peachtree Industrial Blvd., Suite 120
Norcross, GA 30092-3652

Contents

Preface

As we commemorate the 350th anniversary of the Westminster Assembly, let's listen to what our spiritual parents have to tell us. With St. James, let us be "quick to listen, slow to speak" (Jas. 1:19). By again hearing Scripture and the Westminster documents, and by becoming acquainted with the people of the Westminster Assembly, we can better appreciate the foundation that was laid for us and grow in our love for the Lord and his Church—"to Him be glory in the church and in Christ Jesus throughout all generations" (Eph. 3:21).

I would like to thank the following for their help in securing various works on the Westminster Assembly: Sherman Isbell, Reg Barrows, Don Kistler, Joseph Hall, Ligon Duncan, Patrick Baiocchi, Wayne Spear and Dick de Witt. Many thanks also to Will Barker and Tom Patete for their teaching, trust and skill.

I'm most grateful to my wife, Ann, for her love, support and good criticism during this project. This is dedicated to her and my family, in hope that she will not really kill me if I write again. I pray that our covenant children will use this and other studies at the 400th commemoration.

Chronology of the Assembly

1643

12 June	Ordinance by Parliament to call the Assembly
22 June	King's proclamation prohibiting meeting
1 July	Parliament convenes Assembly
12 July–12 Oct.	Committees redraft first 15 of *Thirty-Nine Articles*
17 August	Assembly approves the Solemn League and Covenant
15 September	Scottish Commissioners arrive
25 September	Commons pledges to keep Solemn League and Covenant
12 October	Parliament directs Assembly to work on government; *Thirty-Nine Articles* revision ceases
15 October	House of Lords adopts Solemn League and Covenant

1644

22 April	Directory for Ordination presented to Parliament
24 May	Debate begins on Directory for Public Worship
20 August	Committee for Confession of Faith appointed
8 November	Form of Government sent to Parliament
27 December	Directory for Public Worship presented to Parliament

1645

3 January	Commons approves Directory for Public Worship
23 January	Resolution supporting Presbyterianism passes Commons
7 February	Catechism Committee augmented
12 May	Confession Committee report
7 July	Assembly refers Directory for Church Government
12 September	Assembly approves Rous's Psalms

1646

30 April	Committee from Commons proposes governmental queries
19 July	Death of Twisse; new moderator is Herle
4 December	Confession of Faith (without Scripture proofs) presented to Commons

1647

15 April	Debate on Larger Catechism begins
29 April	Confession of Faith (with Scriptures) presented to Commons
11 May	Confession sent to printer, after review by main committees
5 August	Debate on Shorter Catechism begins
15 October	Larger Catechism completed and submitted to Parliament
25 November	Shorter Catechism presented to Commons

1648

22 March	House of Commons approves Confession
14 April	Catechisms (with Scriptures) presented to Parliament
20 June	House of Lords approves Confession
24 July	House of Commons approves Larger Catechism (never approved by Lords)
25 September	Parliament approves Shorter Catechism

1649

7 February	Both Catechisms ratified by Scottish Estates of Parliament (after approval by the Scottish General Assembly, in summer 1648)
22 February	Last numbered session; adjournment

1652

25 March	Last sitting of Assembly Committee for Examining Ministers

Introduction: Remembering

Just as loss of memory in an individual is a psychiatric defect calling for medical treatment, so too any community which has no social memory is suffering from an illness.[1]

Westminster Abbey in London. If one views this historic church at least two things stand out: pointed spires and elaborate stonework. This gothic structure is more medieval than modern, and strikes us as stately and foreboding.

Intimidated by stony walls and pointed spires, many Christians, even those who attend Reformation-oriented churches, have failed to see inside Westminster, and thus have minimized the value of the work of the Westminster Assembly.

Now, centuries after the Westminster Assembly (1643–49), it is hard to appreciate the Westminster Confession of Faith without knowing something of the historical context in which it was written.

It is important to hear what the Confession has to say. Agreeing with Solomon that "there is nothing new under the sun" (Eccles. 1:9), Christians from the past can instruct those who live today. After all, if the faith was handed down "once for all" (Jude 3), we may expect little change in core biblical truths through the centuries. Since the faith is the same in 1643 or 1993, surely we can learn from other brothers and sisters in Christ.

Let's go back to seventeenth century London and peek in

some of those abbey windows. Some windows will reveal the piety of these Christians. Others will reflect their writings. Another window will focus on the need for and beginning of the Assembly. Still another window will be cracked by the stones of critics, thrown at the time, through the years, and still being hurled today. Another window will emit the light of character, as the strength of Christian living is reflected in certain lives.

A warning, however—some windows will be harder to reach than others. To peer in one window, we can sit idly across the way, and simply view the proceedings with binoculars. Other windows, however, will take a little more effort. We'll have to walk around to the back, or crawl up on a ledge. One window will require us to mount the shoulders of previous friends to gain a glimpse inside. At times, our noses will be smashed against an old window, with our eyes squinting to see what is happening. A few windows will have to be dusted off.

All you'll need is a childlike faith. We may, in the end, be like Peter, Edmund, Susan and Lucy in C.S. Lewis's *The Lion, the Witch, and the Wardrobe.* We may find that Westminster is our wardrobe, a historical yet living tradition that takes us back and that helps us live for today and tomorrow.

Why remember?

Does God want us to remember the past? Does he want us to be encouraged by it?

Nearly 300 variations of the word *remember* appear in the Bible. Remembering is not only commanded, but furthermore is a distinctively helpful tool for Christian living. Often, biblical characters are exhorted to remember how God had already worked faithfully in their lives. This is to remind them that God, who "does not change like shifting shadows" (Jas. 1:17), would remain faithful in the present and the future, just as he had in the past. The biblical logic is that if God was so faithful in the past, and he does not change, then the remembering of his unchanging faithfulness will spur us on to trust him in our own lives, with our own struggles.

From Genesis onward, God selects the word *remember* to emphasize his wholehearted care and providence for his people. God remembers Noah (Gen. 8:1; 9:15), Abraham (19:29) and Rachel (30:22); and to Moses, God specifically remembers his covenant with Abraham (Ex. 2:24; 6:5) as a means of covenant renewal and to inspire Moses' obedience. God also remembers Hannah (1 Sam. 1:19) who yearns for a child.

And when God remembers, he acts, indicating that spiritual remembering is not merely an abstract thought process. God and his people *act* differently if they *remember*. God remembers his covenant with Abraham, Isaac and Jacob (Ex. 32:13) and remembers the land, covenant and ancestors who covenanted with him on earlier occasions (Lev. 26:42, 45). In David's time God remembered his covenant (Ps. 105:8), as he did with Ezekiel (Ezek. 16:60). Even at the birth of Jesus, Zechariah praises God who shows "mercy to our fathers and remembers his holy covenant" (Luke 1:72). God himself frequently remembers.

The Psalms have the greatest concentration of instances of remembering. Some psalms are even classified as "remembering" psalms (Pss. 38 and 70). Imagine, a genre of inspired poetry, whose focus is to bring to remembrance! On several occasions the phrase "praise his holy name" can be translated "give thanks at the *remembrance* of his holiness" (Ps. 30:4; 97:12). And God's righteousness is an enduring remembrance throughout all generations (Ps. 102:12).

Nearly all of Psalm 78 is a retrospective of what God has already done in history. Harking back to the Exodus, following God's chastisement, Israel "remembered that God was their

Rock" (vs. 35), and renewed their trust in him. God also "remembered that they were but flesh, a passing breeze that does not return" (vs. 39), and he extended mercy to them. And then again, in their lapses, "they did not remember his power—the day he redeemed them from the oppressor" (vs. 42).

God *remembers* his love and faithfulness (Ps. 98:3), his holy promise (105:42), his covenant (106:45) and his wonderful works (111:4), while the people often did not remember God's many kindnesses (106:7). The singer asked to be remembered by God when he shows mercy (107:4), and David remembers God's ancient judgments or laws (119:52). As a devotional staple, the Psalmist meditated: "In the night I remember your name [and all that it stands for], O Lord" (119:55). When the people of God remembered better days, they wept (137:1), and the everlasting love of God is associated with the "One who remembered us in our low estate" (136:23).

The prophet Isaiah, in a time of national and spiritual decline, valued remembering. In Isaiah 63:11, as a means of revival, God's people "remembered the days of old, the days of Moses and his people." The Bible reveals a clear connection between revival and remembering.

Earlier, God called on Jacob and Israel to "remember these things" (Is. 44:21), and to rebels God said, "Remember this, fix it in mind....Remember the former things, those of long ago; I am God, and there is no other; I am God, and there is none like me. I make known the end from the beginning, from ancient times, what is still to come" (Is. 46:8–10). Isaiah is consistent with Moses who had sung, "Remember the days of old; consider the generations long past. Ask your father and he will tell you, your elders, and they will explain to you" (Deut. 32:7).

Jonah, in the belly of the fish, found remembering to be vital: "When my life was ebbing away, I remembered you, Lord" (Jon. 2:7). In Malachi 3:16, the people found a written memorial to be helpful: "Then those who feared the Lord talked with each other, and the Lord listened and heard. A scroll of remembrance was written in his presence concerning those who feared the Lord and honored his name."

"Remember how the Lord your God led you" (Deut. 8:2). "Remember the Lord your God, for it is he who gives you the ability to produce wealth, and so confirms his covenant, which he swore to your forefathers" (8:18). "Remember this and never forget how you provoked the Lord...to anger" (9:7). "Do not be afraid of them; remember well what the Lord your God did" (7:18).

In the New Testament, Peter remembers the words of the Lord in Matthew 26:75 and is cut to the heart. The disciples also remember the Lord's teaching (Luke 24:8) and thereby grow in discipleship. Hebrews 10:32 shows the relationship between memory and courage, when the Christians are told to "remember those earlier days after you had received the light, when you stood your ground in great contest in the face of suffering." The aim of that remembering is to "not throw away your confidence; it will be richly rewarded" (10:35); thus memory aids in perseverance (10:36).

Peter, in his epistles, is especially appreciative of the value of remembering how God has acted in the past. In fact the purpose of the second Epistle, according to Peter, is to use remembering "to stimulate you to wholesome thinking" (2 Pet. 3:1). He reminds his readers of already established truths (1:12), thinks "it is right to refresh your memory as long as I live in the tent of this body" (1:13), and commits himself to "every effort to see that...you will always be able to remember these things" (1:15). Evidently, the presbyter/bishop Peter knew the value of remembering for spiritual growth.

John also knew the value of remembering. To the staggering church at Ephesus, the Apostle of Love urges: "Remember the height from which you have fallen! Repent and do the things you did at first" (Rev. 2:5). To the church at Sardis, the one which was in the terminal ward, he said, "Remember, therefore, what you have received and heard; obey it, and repent" (Rev. 3:3).

Memory is reserved for important things in Scripture. Reflect on these other *remembering* passages: Ex. 13:3; 20:8; Esther 9:28; Neh. 4:14; Eccles. 12:1; Luke 22:19; 23:42; Gal. 2:10; 2 Tim. 2:8; Heb. 13:3, 7.

Remembering has always been a potent incentive to regain faithfulness to the Lord. But why remember the work of the Westminster Assembly?

As long as we concentrate on the great working of God's providence in any sector of church history, we can learn lasting lessons.

We do not believe in continuing revelation, but there may be, however, a continuing unfolding of Providence. As we study this segment of history, we ought not expect new re-vealed information, but we can surely see confirmation, or reinforcement for that which has already been revealed in Scripture. Such memorializing is never on par with Scripture, but may serve as a secondary commentary.

If the scriptural principles of the Westminster Assembly were correct, then a remembering of that era is indeed promis-ing. Yet we must constantly preserve the balance between respect for the past and worship of the past. As long as we avoid ancestor worship, this study has great promise. Since all history is God's history, we have nothing to fear. His-Story is useful to God's children in the church, and in daily living.

We need a "rearview mirror" view. When you drive, you may not use your rearview mirror all the time, but whenever checking for bearings, looking for traffic, or considering a lane change, it sure is important.

The history of the Westminster Assembly has great value for us today. One contemporary author, George Grant, summarized: "Remembrance and forgetfulness are the measuring rods of faithfulness throughout the entire canon of Scripture."[2]

To not profit from our own history is one of the surest paths to demise. Alexander Solzhenitsyn put it so well: "To destroy a people you must first sever their roots." This study is our commitment to God-centered renewal.

As observed at the commemoration of the Assembly a century ago, we would do well to affirm: "Ah, the past is never dead! All history is God's mighty electric battery charged to the full with slumbering forces which have subdued kingdoms, overturned thrones, and shaken the world to its center."[3]

Questions for Review.

1. What value do the experiences of Christians who lived in an earlier age have for us today?

2. What Scriptures give us a perspective on the past?

3. Do your own study on the word *remember/remembrance* in the Bible. From a concordance scan, what can you learn?

4. List some of the things that Scripture specifically commands us to remember.

For Discussion.

1. What are some of the ways that older traditions of our faith are treated unfairly or with negative bias in our own day?

2. Why does God place such a premium on remembering? What is the difference between memory, nostalgia and idolatry of the past?

3. What does 2 Timothy 4:1–5 teach us about the attitude of people who do not tolerate sound teaching? How is this related to present gratification?

Spotlight: Thomas Gataker

Thomas Gataker (1574–1654) was the son of a London pastor. Young Thomas enjoyed books. He had a vigorous mind and readily absorbed the principles of the faith. He was a brilliant Greek and Hebrew student.

In 1596 he was appointed a fellow at Sidney College, even before the buildings were completed. At first, he resisted serving as a minister, feeling he was not qualified for the office, but then Gataker preached on the Lord's Day at Everton during his tenure on the Sidney College faculty. In 1603 he received his Bachelor of Divinity degree at Cambridge, but did not proceed to a doctorate for financial reasons.

From 1601 he served ten years as preacher to the Society at Lincoln's Inn in London. He accepted the rectorship at Rotherhithe in Surrey near London following his marriage in 1611. Along with ministering on the Lord's Day, he also established a Friday catechism lecture chiefly designed for the instruction of children and young people.

In 1624 Gataker authored, "A Short Catechism" and *A Discussion of the Popish Doctrine of Transubstantiation*. He studied carefully the theological topic of justification, and later influenced the Westminster Assembly's teaching on justification.

While sitting with the Westminster Assembly during the 1640s, he was offered the Mastership of Trinity College in Cambridge by the Earl of Manchester, but declined. In association with other Westminster Assembly divines, he developed a commentary entitled *English Annotations Upon All the Books of the Old and New Testaments*, writing the commentaries on Isaiah, Jeremiah and Lamentations. A collected edition of his sermons was published in 1637 and of his Latin works in 1698.

Although one of the most respected thinkers of his time, Gataker also was a very practical man. Upon his retirement from the ministry, he conducted catechism classes for the students who stayed in his home. In addition Gataker was a generous man, giving his alms in secret. In his will he left £50 to the poor of his parish, £50 to ten ministers who were in poor financial condition, and £5 each to eight ministers' widows.

Simeon Ashe records Gataker's dying words:

I am now conflicting with my last adversary, though I believe the sting is taken out. Nature will struggle, but I humbly submit unto the good pleasure of God. I heartily beg the pardon of my many sins, especially of my want of…fidelity in my public and private charge, hoping to be washed with Christ's blood, and desiring to be translated out of this restless condition. I expect daily, yea hourly to be translated into that everlasting rest, which God hath prepared for them who are interested in his Christ. And I pray God to bless you, and his whole ministry every where.

Gataker gives a lasting example of a pious blend of scholarship and holiness. He is remembered as a man of great intellect and as an excellent pastor, a loving father and generous giver.

1. Origins of the Assembly

> History must be our deliverer not only from the undue influence of other times, but from the undue influence of our own, from the tyranny of environment and the pressures of the air we breathe.[1]

History doesn't unfold in a vacuum. Events don't spring from nothing. The Westminster Assembly, too, had a history that shaped it.

When the Westminster Assembly met in the seventeenth century, the world was a different place. Only recently had North America been colonized. The mind-set of the Westminster Assembly participants (those who studied divinity or theology were called divines) was closer to medieval chivalry than to our modern rights-oriented thinking.

If one could have stood at the highest window of Westminster Abbey on that July morning in 1643, one would have seen an impressive procession of lords, lawyers, pastors and teachers as they gathered for the opening Convocation of the Assembly. As these scholars assembled, all their varied influences streamed together, like the confluence of numerous rivers.

The Westminster Assembly had its roots in the Reformation. God raised up leading reformers in the sixteenth century—Martin Luther in Germany, John Calvin and Ulrich Zwingli in Switzerland and John Knox in Scotland. While these early reformers agreed on core theological truths, there was little consensus on many other practical questions. As a result the Reformed churches in France, Holland, Hungary, England and Scotland had significant differences.

John Knox, exiled from Scotland during the reign of Bloody Mary, found Calvin's Geneva to be one of the most perfect embodiments of Christian teaching anywhere. He took those Reformation truths back to Scotland in the late 1550s.

In England, a native British Reformed church was formed when Henry VIII broke from Rome in 1543. In the early days of this Anglican church, under Henry's children Edward VI and Elizabeth I, two doctrinal statements (the *Forty-Two Articles* and the *Thirty-Nine Articles*) proved to be forerunners of the Westminster Confession of Faith.

In England, the crown officially supported the state church, and it was difficult to follow through on reforms. The Anglican church, although Reformed in doctrine, retained many practices of the Roman Catholic Church. But, as the Scriptures were taught and translated, Christians in England, particularly those who had been exposed to the teachings of Calvin on the continent, began to yearn to continue their reforms, just as Christians in Europe had. These people were called non-Conformists, Dissenters or Puritans. Most of the participants at the Westminster Assembly were from this group. The late sixteenth century saw Reformation theology take the English universities by storm. Some of the greatest teachers and preachers in this age were early Presbyterians.

In 1572 the first English presbytery was established under the leadership of the Father of English Presbyterianism, Thomas Cartwright (1535–1603). This presbytery had as many as 500 ministers, some of whom were outstanding leaders in the land. At the turn of the seventeenth century, Presbyterianism was becoming increasingly popular. Although this was rapidly becoming the people's faith, it was perceived as a dangerous threat to the bishops and to the monarch who appointed them.

Though trampled by the crown, Presbyterianism kept growing. Despite the opposition of King James I and his son Charles I, who clearly saw the democratic goals of Presbyterianism as a threat to their "divine right," the ground swell of Reformed believers in the British Isles nearly demanded an Assembly.

By the early 1640s there was, in England, strife over the impact of the Reformation faith. The unity of Britain was at stake and the need for Reformed Christians to unite and work together was never greater. Fortunately, rather than the independent-mindedness so prevalent today, Christians admired the work of other Christians. This led to the desire to counsel with one another.

In 1641, London ministers, smarting under the tyranny of the episcopacy, petitioned Parliament to convene a "free synod, to take into consideration and remove the grievances of the Church."[2] King Charles, hoping to appease the moderate Protestants, allowed a Religion Committee to serve Parliament in March of that year. Many of the men who would later become participants in the Westminster Assembly took part in these and other convocations.

In May 1641, the Root and Branch Petition (calling for the elimination, root and branch, of a Bishop-ruled church) was submitted, angering the king. Later, in November 1641, the Grand Remonstrance, which contained 204 clauses, was presented to the king (clause 185 specifically called for a synod of pious, learned and judicious divines to meet and to deliberate on which measures would be most helpful for the "peace and good government of the church"). He promptly rejected it. In December it was twice resubmitted and twice vetoed.

By May 1642, Parliament had done everything necessary

for convening the Assembly, yet still the king stalled. The Assembly was originally scheduled to meet on July 1, 1642, but due to the king's opposition did not meet until a year later. In July 1642, the House of Commons called for the Assembly to meet, even though delayed, and in August 1642 Charles renewed his threats against any who attended. In October 1642 there was yet another bill calling for the Assembly, but still Charles vetoed it. The bill lapsed, and the king refused to give his assent to a total of six of these bills. His decision was finally overridden in 1643.

The king, as would be expected from the head of the Church of England, condemned any such synod on June 22, 1643.

The original ordinance was clear in its aims; it read:

Whereas, amongst the infinite blessings of Almighty God upon this nation, none is nor can be more dear unto us than the purity of our religion; and for that, as yet, many things remain in the liturgy, discipline, and government of the church, which do necessarily require a further and more perfect reformation, than as yet hath been obtained; and whereas, it hath been declared and resolved by the Lords and Commons assembled in Parliament, that the present church government, by archbishops, bishops, their chancellors, commissars, deans, and chapters, arch-deacons, and other ecclesiastical officers, depending upon the hierarchy, is evil, and justly offensive and burdensome to the kingdom, a great impediment to reformation and growth of religion, and very prejudicial to the state and government of this kingdom; and, therefore, they are resolved, that the same shall be taken away, and that such a government shall be settled in the church, as may be most agreeable to God's holy word, and most apt to procure and preserve the peace of the church at home, and nearer agreement with the church of Scotland, and other Reformed churches abroad; and for the better effecting hereof, and for the vindicating and clearing of the doctrine of the church of England from all false calumnies and aspersions, it is thought fit and necessary, to call an assembly of learned, godly, and judicious divines, who, together with some members of both houses of Parliament, are to consult and advise of such matters and things, touching the premises, as shall be proposed unto them, by both or either of the houses of Parliament, and to give their advice and counsel therein, to both or either of the said houses, when, and as often, as they shall be thereunto required.[3]

The ordinance directed that the divines meet in King Henry VII's chapel at Westminster beginning July 1, 1643 with two tasks: (1) to set down the biblical patterns of the Reformation faith in the areas of liturgy (worship form) and polity (church government), and (2) to defend such Reformation distinctives from attack. These assemblymen were latter-day Nehemiahs, armed with trowels in one hand to rebuild the temple, and bearing swords in the other to defend from attack.

Beginning Organization

The Assembly opened on Saturday, July 1, 1643 in the Abbey Church in Westminster, with William Twisse, the Parliament-appointed moderator, preaching from John 14:18 on the text of "I will not leave you comfortless." Immediately following the sermon, the divines adjourned to King Henry VII's Chapel where between 60 and 70 delegates answered the roll call to begin the convocation.

This Assembly was frequently reminded of its potential significance. At the end of the first week, the members were exhorted by Matthew Newcomen to

> keep no silence, give the Lord no rest until He establish the house....except the Lord build the house, reform the Church, it is to no purpose to go about to reform it....I need not tell you how many eyes and expectations there are upon this Assembly....what you pray for, contend for...as you pray that God would establish his Church in peace, so labor to work out the Church's peace. And lastly, as you pray that God would make the Church a praise, so endeavor that also; endeavoring...that all her ways may be ordered according to the rule of God's Word: that the Gospel may run and be glorified: that those two great illuminating ordinances of Preaching and Catechizing, which are as the greater and lesser lights of heaven, may have such liberty, encouragement, maintenance, that all the earth may be filled with the knowledge of the Lord.[4]

One of the earliest adopted procedures exhibited the highest regard for Scripture as the only infallible source for the final products of the Assembly. Each commissioner, one week after the opening, vowed: "I do seriously and solemnly protest, in the presence of Almighty God, that in this Assembly, whereof I am a member, I will not maintain anything in matters of doctrine, but what I think in my conscience to be truth; or, in point of discipline, but what I shall conceive to conduce most to the glory of God, and the good and peace of his church."[5]

This group desired to be guided by the Reformation motto: *sola scriptura* (by Scripture alone). This vow was renewed frequently to remind the participants of their original obligation to be nothing but scriptural.

The first order of business among these good Presbyterians was to divide the membership into committees. Although our experiences with committees leads us to mock such as often being more cumbersome than helpful, these godly men believed that if members were working together for the Lord's glory, the whole would be greater than the sum of its parts. Hence the Assembly was divided into three committees to revise the *Thirty-Nine Articles,* the doctrinal standard of the Church of England.

Later, other committees were set up to prepare the confession and the catechisms. The design of all these layers of committees and discussions was to insure that biblical opinions served as iron-sharpening-iron. "There is wisdom in many counselors" (Prov. 15:22) was well heeded in this case. The result would be a document that the church could trust, and one that was freer from the bias, partisanship and imbalance of many subsequent statements.

The assemblymen did most of their work in a richly paneled room about 20 feet by 40 feet. At the head of the room, on a raised platform, sat the moderator, William Twisse. Behind him were large windows which served as the primary source of light. In front of the moderator at floor level were seated the two vice-moderators (assessors), Cornelius Burgess and John White. Running the length of the room was a narrow table at the head of which sat the clerks, Adoniram Byfield and Henry Roborough. Ranks of risers surrounded the narrow table. The lowest rank seated 5, with successive rows seating 7, 9 or 11. This room could accommodate at most 100 people.

In light of the desire of the participants for the outcome to be as ecumenical as possible, shortly after convening, the Assembly sent a delegation to Scotland seeking to secure the cooperation of the Scottish leaders. A company of lords and divines were sent to Scotland bearing a letter from the English Parliament, lamenting that they were "ready to be swallowed up by Satan and his instrument." Parliament implored the Scottish church to send some delegates to help "serve God with one consent, and stand up against antichrist, as one man."[6] Seven Scots were sent to serve as advisers.

The proposed framework of agreement was the Solemn League and Covenant which the Scottish church had previously adopted. To further uniformity, the Scottish leaders asked the English Parliament to approve the same covenant as a condition for sending the advisers (as well as the Scottish army which the English were particularly anxious to see in the field). The English Parliament readily agreed to these terms. So significant was this event that it is recorded as being met with applause, "bursting into tears of a deep, full, and sacred joy" and was estimated by one participant to be a "new period and crisis of the most great affair which these hundred years has exercised."[7]

Some of the commitments spelled out in the Solemn League and Covenant show how the Assembly itself would conclude some major issues. For example, the signers of this document vowed to work for the "preservation of the reformed religion...doctrine, worship, discipline, and government, according to the word of God, and the example of the best reformed churches." Moreover, they pledged themselves to the "extirpation of Popery, Prelacy, superstition, heresy, schism, profaneness, and whatsoever shall be found to be contrary to sound doctrine."[8]

The Assembly's initial assignment was to revise the *Thirty-Nine Articles*. Ten weeks into this project, however, the articles were set aside and serious work began on what was to become the Westminster Confession of Faith (WCF). In October 1643, Parliament directed the Assembly to write the Directory for Public Worship, and with the arrival of the Scottish Commissioners, the Assembly totally abandoned the *Thirty-Nine Articles* revision.

From Scripture we see that the earliest patterns of biblical government show Christians from a region meeting together to solve disputes (e.g., Acts 15). The seventeenth-century leaders at Westminster saw themselves through the windows of this and other Scriptures.

According to Scripture, God has made us so that we can learn from Christians who have gone before us. Most of Hebrews 11 reviews the faithfulness of the Old Testament saints. Stephen, in Acts 7, does the same thing while facing fierce opposition.

Romans 15:4 teaches that the past has great value for present and future Christian living: "For everything that was written in the past was written to teach us [today], so that through endurance and the encouragement of the Scriptures we might have hope." Thus, the remembering of God's past, contains promise to engender endurance, encouragement and hope.

Observe the context of that well-known verse, 1 Corinthians 10:13. Verses 1–5 of chapter 10 speak of the believers in Moses' time as sharing the same spiritual dynamics as we today. Verse 6 reads, "Now these things [in the past] occurred as examples to keep us from setting our hearts on evil things as they did." Note, the past is our kind instructor, providing examples "if we have ears to hear" to assist us in avoiding evil.

Verse 11 continues: "These things happened to them as examples and were written down as warnings for us, on whom the fulfillment of the ages has come. So, if you think you are standing firm, be careful that you do not fall!" Then, with that context in mind, with the value of historical example underscored, we are comforted (as we remember the past and God's faithfulness) that indeed, "No temptation has seized you except what is common to man. And God is faithful; He will not let you be tempted beyond what you can bear. But when you are tempted, he will also provide a way out so that you can stand up under it" (1 Cor. 10:13).

Questions for Review.

1. In less than 60 seconds, can you give a setting for the Westminster Assembly, beginning with the Reformation?

2. Review the language of the various bills, petitions, ordinances and covenants (especially the Solemn League and Covenant) considered by Parliament from 1640–1643. What do these tell us about the people's beliefs at the time?

3. Can order, say in parliamentary order, be bad? Is it always frustrating for the growth of the church and evangelism, or is there ever a place for doing things "in a fitting and orderly way" (1 Cor.14:40)?

4. Review Hebrews 11 and Acts 7 to see how a knowledge of the past is useful for the present?

5. Study your Bibles to see if any confessions or creeds are contained in the Scriptures.

For Discussion.

1. What Proverbs could be useful in setting procedure? That is, if you were convening an Assembly, what kind of procedural guidelines could you find in the book of Proverbs, to help insure fairness and truth?

2. Isn't piety always squelched by formality? What makes the difference?

3. Find a copy of the *Thirty-Nine Articles* and compare sections with the WCF. Or read parts of some other post-Reformation creed, and discuss.

Spotlight: Thomas Case

Thomas Case was the son of a minister in the County of Kent in England. His early training in the faith led him to write: "The importance of early instruction is written upon the whole system of nature, and repeated in every page of the history of Providence. You may bend a young twig and make it receive almost any form; but that which has attained to maturity, and taken its ply, you will never bring into another shape than that which it naturally bears....Children may undoubtedly receive much benefit by the use of means, in a very early period of life. And when parents use the means, they ought carefully to remember the beautiful connection between the duty and the promise."

As a youth, he learned that prayer is one of the mainstays of the Christian life, the very breath of regenerate persons. In 1616 he became a student at Oxford where he graduated with his Masters in 1623. He was a lecturer and later the pastor of Mary Magdalen Church in Milk Street, London.

A pioneer of organized morning prayer exercises, Thomas Case solicited prayer requests for the various needs in the city. He and a number of other ministers agreed to spend a half hour in the morning in prayer, and another half in an exhortation. Great fruit blossomed from these prayer ministries.

As were the other Assembly divines, Case was frequently asked to preach to the Parliament on public occasions. In preparation for adopting the Solemn League and Covenant (1643), he preached several sermons to his congregation admonishing,

> To every soul that shall enter into this holy league and covenant; my request is, that they would look around them: life and death is before them; if we break with God now, we have just cause to fear, God will stand

to covenant no more with us, but will avenge the quarrel, with our utter destruction; if we be sincere and faithful, this covenant will be a foundation of much peace, joy, glory, and security, to us, and our seed, to the coming of Christ, which that it may be, shall be the earnest prayer of him, who is thy servant for Jesus' sake.

As both an ardent Presbyterian and a man of conscience, Case was ejected from his pastoral charge—and even imprisoned for a time—when he refused an "engagement" to support the government of Oliver Cromwell, apart from the king and House of Lords. Subsequently, until the Restoration, he served as lecturer in Giles-in-the-Fields.

Following the Westminster Assembly, Case was a representative at the Savoy Conference (1661), and in 1662 he was silenced with his brothers by the Act of Uniformity or the Great Ejection. He died at the age of 84 in 1682.

In his farewell sermon, Case lamented the lack of spirituality in England at the time: "In things of the world we are all in all, and all in every part...but in prayer, how many things are we doing?" He decried the absence of concern for Christians in other places: "When did we go to bed sick for the afflictions of God's people abroad? When did their miseries cost us an hour's sleep? or a meal's meat? When did we lie in the dust, and cry out, Ah Lord! their glory! Because we have not shed tears for their blood, God may justly say, 'The next turn of persecution shall be yours.'"

2. Parties, Procedures and Politics

> We do not claim for them perfection or infallibility.
> They were men; and were subject to human infir-
> mities, and were infected with some of the preju-
> dices of the age in which they lived, which is more
> or less true of all men.[1]

The Assembly was not a homogenous group. There were three major participating parties. They were, from largest to smallest, the Presbyterians, Independents and Erastians. The Episcopalians attended until the king forbade it.

There were debates, disagreements (one esteemed member was even suspended for a time because of his outburst), political maneuvering, and procedural hurdles. (Times haven't changed that much.)

This window is around the back of Westminster Abbey. As we look inside, it will be as if we have stumbled upon a series of secret meetings. The various sides, including Parliament, each have their strategies and agenda. This Assembly is peopled by real human beings, who desire the reform of the church. Yet they don't always agree on method.

Parties

The first Erastians adopted a medical doctor, Thomas Erastus (1524–1583), as their patron saint. This system gave final authority, even in church matters, only to the state. According to one historian, the chief principle of Erastianism was the "all-supremacy of the State. The Church was a mere department of the State; the pastoral office was simply persuasive; ministers had no power to excommunicate or punish."[2]

The chief proponents of this view at the Assembly were Selden, Lightfoot, Coleman and Whitaker, all formidable exponents, but very much in the minority. Erastianism never enjoyed much support in post-Westminster Presbyterianism. The predominant Erastian churches in our time are in Europe or Asia (such as the state churches of Sweden or Germany).

In the debate against the esteemed and brilliant Erastian, Selden, 30-year-old George Gillespie saw the issue clearly, and assessed the pathology of Erastianism, for all to understand:

> Erastianism…has not the honor of being descended from honest parents. The *father* of it is the *old serpent*; its mother is the enmity of our nature against the kingdom of our Lord Jesus Christ; and the midwife, who brought this unhappy brood into the light of the world, was Thomas Erastus….The Erastian error being born, the breasts which gave it suck were *profaneness* and *self-interest*; its strong food, when advanced in growth, was arbitrary government; and its careful tutor was Arminianism.[3]

The second group, slightly larger than the Erastians, but still vastly outnumbered, were the Independents who declared that "every particular congregation of Christians has an entire and complete power of jurisdiction over its members to be exercised by the elders thereof within itself."[4]

The Independents were responsible for the most challenging and time-consuming debate. Although they were Reformed in their theological sentiments, this group did not affirm the strong connectionalism advocated by the Presbyterians. Independents and Presbyterians, both anti-Romanist and anti-bishop, would be united in a great many aspects of faith and life. But on important governmental points, they disagreed.

The Independents were strong-minded, frequently trying the patience of the Assembly. Baillie called them obstructionists, "our great retarders," who "debated all things too prolixie [they were verbose] which came within twenty miles of their quarters."[5]

In the century leading up to 1643, the growth of Presbyterianism had been remarkable. Prior to 1543 the only recognized church in the British Isles was the Roman Catholic church, with its episcopal form of government. When Henry VIII left the Roman church, the Church of England was born— Reformed in doctrine, but hierarchical in government, i.e., the bishops answered to the Archbishop of Canterbury, who answered to the monarch.

In the late sixteenth century, with the rise of Puritanism at Cambridge, Presbyterianism (with rule by representative elders) appeared. It was officially repudiated, yet, in spite of this, a mere half-century later, the majority of the Westminster Assembly were ardent Presbyterians.

Mitchell suggested two reasons for the victory of Presbyterianism at the Westminster Assembly. First, it is impossible to overestimate the influence of the Scottish Presbyterian commissioners on the Assembly. Young Gillespie was "more than a match for all the learned Erastians and Independents in the Assembly."[6]

The second reason is more political and pragmatic. There could be no compromise for the divines who believed that Presbyterianism is the revealed plan of organization for God's church, given as a divine mandate. The Assembly realized that to move ahead, it would have to accept the Presbyterian form of government.

The Presbyterian victory at the Assembly is evidenced in the end results—the Westminster Confession of Faith, a clearly Presbyterian document, which in many respects became the mother of later Presbyterian policies.

"They harangue long and very learnedly"

Watching some of the debates through a rear window provides an unusual perspective on the Assembly. There was little of the showmanship and sensationalism so prevalent in today's debating forums. One historian notes,

> No pygmies contended there. It was a battle of Titans. The High Church Presbyterians of the Cartwright School, backed by the Scotch Commissioners, argued with splendid ability and genius for the Presbyterian form of government and the divine rights of Presbytery. They resorted to no quibbles, or sophistries, or intrigues, inside or outside of the Chamber, to gain their ends. They drew their weapons from the Word of God, and wielded them with a skill and mastery which the opposition, with Parliament on their side, could not overcome.[7]

While substance was the target of these debates, the process to reach agreement on that substance should not be forgotten or minimized. Early in the Assembly, a set of guidelines were adopted by Parliament for the Assembly's debates. Some features of these bylaws follow:

1. Vice-Moderators were appointed to take the place of the Moderator upon absence or illness.

2. Two clerks who were not members of the Assembly (to insure non-partisanship and objectivity) were to take minutes.

3. Every member must take a solemn vow from the outset "not to maintain anything but what he believes to be the truth, in sincerity." This was a self-consciously biblical group, who desired to be guided by scripturally informed consciences seeking to please God. Moreover, this vow was read afresh at the beginning of each week, on Monday morning to remind the participants that they had a continuing obligation to remain scriptural.

4. No proposal was to be discussed the first day it was introduced. These experienced men realized the tendency to be railroaded into unwise action if not given proper time to reflect on weighty proposals.

5. "What any man undertakes to prove as necessary, he shall make good out of Scripture."

6. Assembly participants must submit to the Moderator, unless supported by the majority of the Assembly.

7. The right and privilege to present a dissenting opinion with reasons along with such appeal being sent to both houses of Parliament for their consideration.

8. Upon reading the final version of the motion, if the majority agree, such shall be entered as the judgment of the Assembly.

This Assembly, then, like any parliamentary body, had rules, bylaws and procedures for the orderly dispatch of business. Any presbytery, synod or general assembly today is organized similarly.

Most debate was conducted in a gentlemanly manner

much like modern senators addressing one another as "distinguished Senators." Baillie described the debates:

> Every committee…in the afternoon meeting prepares matters for the Assembly; sets down their minds in distinct propositions, and backs their propositions with texts of Scripture. After the prayer, Mr. Byfield, the scribe, reads the proposition and Scriptures, whereupon the Assembly debates in a most grave and orderly way. No man is called up to speak but who stands up of his own accord. He speaks so long as he will without interruption….They harangue long and very learnedly. They study the question well beforehand, and prepare their speeches; but withal, the men are exceeding prompt, and well spoken. I do marvel at the very accurate and extemporal replies that many of them usually make. When upon every proposition, and on every text of Scripture that is brought to confirm it, every man who will has said his whole mind, and the replies, and duplies, and triplies, are heard, then the most part calls, "To the question."[8]

The fullest opportunity was given for debate. There were occasions when the majority even delayed a vote, even though sure of carrying its point, so that the decisions might be as acceptable as possible to everyone involved. "One is compelled to admire that spirit of conciliation and of confidence in the power of truth which determined the policy of the body as a whole."[9]

One historian of the Assembly noted: "In general, the debates were deliberate and learned; and the speakers treated each other with great courtesy and deference; but sometimes they became not only warm, but hot…and in one instance, the Assembly was thrown into hubbub and confusion, while Dr. Burgess was speaking."[10]

In another place Baillie indicates that at times the Assembly was bogged down, when he writes, "We have been…in a pitiful labyrinth these twelve days about Ruling Elders."[11]

Politics

This Assembly was no freer from politics than any other assembly. One wag has described the heart of Presbyterianism as "wherever two are more are gathered, there also are politics." Through the rear windows, we can glimpse some of the political moves, such as attempts at the outset to recruit the Scottish commissioners to aid in eliminating prelacy (hierarchical government), the contest of wills between Parliament and the Assembly to define proper roles of authority, the efforts of the Independents to garner more public acceptance, and even the possible use of procedural delays in the most pious of forms.

It was not above Parliament to convene the Assembly to assist it in the overthrow of the king. There were numerous members of Parliament who, although not believing in the Reformation, nonetheless wanted change in the political administration. This party was ruled by political, not religious, convictions. They knew that most of the public preferred the old faith to the new, so they supported only those changes essential to the Protestant faith. Political motives were present even before the Assembly convened.

Parliament quickly allied itself with the divines, as opposed to the monarchy and the Church of England. As King Charles I summed up accurately, "King and prelate on the one side, against Parliament and Puritan on the other."[12] As these two parties began to draw the lines, the divines also realized that when they convened they put their livings, as well as their lives, on the line.

There was also division between the Independents and the

Presbyterians. Francis Patton noted,

> A jealousy sprung up between the army and the
> Parliament. Republican sentiments prevailed among
> the Puritan soldiers. The doctrine of the Indepen-
> dents suited their democratic proclivities. A growing
> jealousy of Scotland and estrangement from their
> Northern allies prejudiced them more and more
> against Presbyterianism, and deepened their partial-
> ity for Independence. Some rash measures of Parlia-
> ment, adopted in haste to restrain the alarming in-
> crease of heresy and promote uniformity, gave rise to
> a loud clamor in favor of toleration and against imagi-
> nary persecution.[13]

Another aspect of political reality was the role of the
Scottish commissioners, and their bartering to have their covenant adopted at the outset of the Assembly. The Scots' gaining
a pre-commitment to abide by Solemn League and Covenant
was a brilliant political stroke for Presbyterianism (perhaps
largely attributable to Alexander Henderson). With the outbreak of the Civil War in 1643, the Independents in Parliament
realized they needed an ally. The Scots were the best and
quickest hope. One historian interpreted: "It looks as if the
Scotch did a little trading. They promised aid on condition that
the Presbyterians of Scotland should have some representation
in the Westminster Assembly and all members of Parliament
would sign a solemn League and Covenant to be drawn up by
the Scotch."[14]

Some have theorized that the original assignment to amend
the *Thirty-Nine Articles* was a delaying tactic from the outset,
conceived to allow time for the Scottish commissioners to
arrive.

On another front, Parliament wanted to be sure that the
divines did their assigned job without getting out of control. It

soon became apparent that Parliament would have a difficult time both feeding *and* taming this tiger. Parliament was displeased that the divines repeatedly spoke of government as by divine rule, rather than as being permitted by the civil government, in that this leached over into Parliament's turf. Parliament appointed some laymen to the assembly because, as Selden put it, "There must be some laymen in the Synod to overlook the Clergy, lest they spoil the Civil work; just as when the good woman puts a cat into the milk house to kill a mouse, she sends her maid to look after the cat, lest the cat eat up the cream."[15]

Parliament and the Assembly were politically related. Briefly, Presbyterian polity was even favored in England. While the Scottish presbyters desired even greater freedom from the state, even this mild form of Presbyterianism led to such an outcry, that the Parliament voted to burn what they deemed the Scottish amendments by the "hands of the common hangman."[16]

The Assembly met for five and a half years—1,163 sessions—before adjourning on February 22, 1649. It has, indeed, left its mark on western civilization.

Questions for Review.

1. Why is church government important? Does Scripture treat it as important?

2. Briefly summarize the tenets of (a) Erastians, (b) Episcopalians, (c) Independents, (d) Presbyterians

3. What can you learn about how to treat one another from this chapter?

4. Search for biblical examples of public debate over critical

matters (Hint: Acts 15). What role does debate have in our churches? How can it help? What should our attitude be toward disagreements?

5. Are churches free from politics? Are there biblical principles that guide such endeavors?

For Discussion.

1. Do a study on factions, parties and heresies in Scripture. What does the New Testament teach about these?

2. Is it always the case that those who call for Christian unity are free from erecting doctrinal barriers to that unity?

Spotlight: Jeremiah Burroughs

Jeremiah Burroughs (1599–1646) was one of the many Assembly leaders educated at Cambridge. Despite the persecution under Bishop Wren and Archbishop Laud, Burroughs consistently protested against the state church, even temporarily undergoing self-exile, relocating to Holland where he became minister of an English church in Rotterdam. Upon returning to England he served as pastor in two of the largest congregations in London. He was an Independent who maintained candor, modesty and charity.

In preaching, he did not use "those gaudy ornaments which too often put the preacher in the place of his text; or, as one has well expressed it, serve only to evaporate weighty truths, and to make them appear as light as the style. His great aim was to guide his hearers in the way to heaven; and accordingly, plainness and persuasion were the chief objects of his attention. The plain Calvinistic doctrine of the Reformation was honored with wonderful success, in promoting the interests of the Redeemer's kingdom, at that time."

Jeremiah Burroughs was an "esteemed and great ornament of the pulpit" and was known as the morning star of Stepney, the large congregation he pastored. He also wrote on difficult subjects with uncommon evangelical piety. Cotton Mather, a patriarch of American Christianity, gave great praise for Burroughs, who died at 47 on November 14, 1646. He was known as an excellent scholar, a good expositor and a popular preacher.

Burroughs has a lasting witness through many of his writings. He was known for his four-volume practical commentary on Hosea, and for numerous sermons preached at public thanksgivings and before the House of Peers and the House of Lords in the 1640s. He authored a devotional guide of 754 pages on Hebrews 11:25, 26, *Moses his Choice, with his eye fixed upon Heaven: discovering the happy condition of a self-denying heart.*

He was so grieved by divisions among Independents and Presbyterians that in later life he wrote a plea for unity among Christians. Burroughs is also known for his *The Saints' Treasury*, his sermons on the Beatitudes, *The Saints' Happiness* (both recently reprinted) and *The Rare Jewel of Christian Contentment.*

3. The Players

In the Westminster Assembly we may behold Calvinism putting on the whole armor of God, likewise taking the shield of faith and the sword of the Spirit, and going forth unto the final battle against the Church of Rome.[1]

Y ou can't tell the players without a program" is true not only in sports, but also in terms of understanding our history. History is, after all, *human* history.

This window is an easy one to look through. Just stand on ground level, and look through it. That is, in fact, what a number of members of Parliament did—they came to watch and to listen. An acquaintance with the members of the gathering will help us appreciate the teaching of the Assembly.

There were a total of 151 commissioned members of the Westminster Assembly. Most were nominated by knights or burgesses from districts, who were familiar with the life, views, and ministry of those nominated. Several groups constituted the Assembly.

The largest group was, as expected of a theological assembly, the divines (ministers). Most members had been ordained as pastors, but there were also many who were professors of religion. Many were famous. Some are profiled at the end of chapters. In this chapter, several will be sketched in some detail.

The Assembly also had 21 representatives from the House

of Commons; these might find their parallel in today's ruling elders. One of the leaders among these, who might be known as ruling elders today, was John Selden, who is frequently reported as taking a leading part in debate during the Assembly. There was also a father-son team, Sirs Henry Vane Senior and Junior, both attorneys. Other laymen included: John Glynne, Recorder of London; Matthew Hale, later Chief Justice of the King's Bench; John White, a Vice-Moderator for the Assembly; and John Wallis, the eminent mathematician. This lay group was talented, experienced and moderate.

The average attendance at the sessions was about half of the total body. Some 20 to 30 never or seldom attended, because of their loyalty to Anglicanism.

The members of the Assembly were leaders in their fields. Among the respected professors in their midst were Herbert Palmer of Queen's College, Cambridge; Joshua Hoyle, Regius Professor of Divinity, Oxford; Thomas Goodwin, later a professor at Magdalen College, Oxford; John Arrowsmith and his successor, Anthony Tuckney, professors of Divinity at Cambridge; Richard Vines, professor at Pembroke Hall, Cambridge. Cambridge graduates numbered 68; Oxford graduates, 48.

The Erastian Selden was described as "a living library and a walking study....when questions arose as to language, law, antiquity or precedent, Selden was practically master of the situation."[2] William Gouge, besides being a scholar, was for 35 years the preacher at Blackfriars Church, London. During his tenure, the church became so famous that visitors to London did not consider their business finished until they had heard a sermon there. The last surviving member was a young man at the Assembly, an eminent mathematician, John Wallis, whose hand played a large role in crafting the wording of the Shorter Catechism.

Here are short biographies of four of the more prominent

assembly participants. William Twisse was English, the other three, Scottish.

William Twisse

The man who became the first moderator of the Assembly had a long and distinguished career in ministry. Described as a "venerable man, with [a] long, pale countenance, imposing beard, lofty brow, and meditative eye," he has often been miscast, or remained unknown. William Twisse of Newbury was a scholar, and devout man of God. Shortly after the Long Parliament took power (Nov. 3, 1640), the members called for a preliminary briefing with learned divines. Among the participants in this warm-up for the Assembly were Archbishop Ussher and William Twisse. Thus, even before the Assembly, Twisse had established his reputation as one of the leading theologians of his day. He was known as a deep and often speculative genius. Baxter describes him as "a man very famous for his Scholastical Wit and Writings in a very smooth triumphant style."

In addition, his potency as a controversialist and defender of the Reformed faith was widely known. Fuller described him as "a divine of great abilities, learning, piety, and moderation....His plain preaching was good, his disputing better, his pious living best of all....Good with the trowel, but better with the sword, more happy in polemical divinity than edifying doctrine."[3] He was theologically precise but a true peacemaker devoid of that quarrelsomeness that so often accompanies depth of theological conviction.

Twisse was known for his own prayer life and family devotionals. One biographer reports that "always before dinner...he read a portion of the Holy Scriptures, expounding the more obscure and difficult passages, for the edification of the family...that their souls might be refreshed along with their bodies; that they might see themselves in the glass of the divine law; become better acquainted with the Word of God...and talk of all his wondrous works."

According to participant Robert Baillie, Twisse was an excellent and even-handed moderator. Even if appointed by those "who guide most matters for their own interests,"[4] Twisse proved a valuable gift to fairness and efficiency. He is described by Baillie as one who "the world knows, is very learned in the questions he has studied...very good, and beloved of all, and highly esteemed."

Not one to seek prominence, Twisse humbly thought himself better suited for other tasks. "Unskilled in parliamentary law, diffident of his own judgment, incapable of strong self-assertion, dreamy and absent-minded in the midst of the long debates, he strove to do his duty in an office which he would have been only too glad to demit."[5] When it is recalled that Twisse was a strict Calvinist, and yet that the Confession does not reflect his particular views, it becomes clear that he was a moderator who did not seek to inject his own personal views on the Assembly. This should serve as a potent rebuttal to those who accuse the Assembly of intolerance.

Witherspoon reports that Twisse died while praying, and upon hearing that his end was near, he smiled with confidence and said, "Now, at length, I shall have leisure to follow my studies to all eternity."[6]

George Gillespie

George Gillespie, a Scot, was the youngest member of the Assembly and also one of the shortest lived. Born in 1613 to John Gillespie, a minister at Kirkcaldy, he began his academic studies in 1629 at St. Andrews. Being convinced at an early age that episcopacy was a human invention, he courageously refused Episcopal ordination. As early as 1637 he authored his first book, *A Dispute against the English Popish Ceremonies*, which quickly established Gillespie as an astute theological mind and a force to be reckoned with. In this work, he systematically and biblically refuted the Episcopal claims point by point.

Shortly thereafter, the power of the bishops waned, and Gillespie was ordained by the Presbytery of Kirkcaldy on April 26, 1638. Fittingly, he was the first to be admitted by a presbytery in that period without ordination by bishops, courageously practicing what he preached. In 1642 he moved to Edinburgh to accept a call, and arrived at the Westminster Assembly with Henderson in the first rank of Scottish Presbyterians in September 1643, at the age of 30.

Of Gillespie, Robert Baillie said:

That is an excellent youth; my heart blessed God in his behalf. There is no man whose parts in public dispute I do so admire. He has studied so accurately all the points that are yet come to our Assembly; he has got so ready, so assured, so solid a way of public debating; that however there be in the Assembly divers excellent men, yet, in my poor judgment, there is not one who speaks more rationally, and to the point, than that brave youth has done ever; so that his absence would be prejudicial to our whole cause, and unpleasant to all here that wishes it well.[7]

Gillespie authored some major works in Presbyterian polity, and in 1647 when the Scottish Assembly adopted the Westminster Confession of Faith, they also printed Gillespie's *One Hundred and Eleven Propositions*, which were aimed at refuting Erastianism. The following year, at 35, Gillespie was elected moderator of the Scottish Assembly. It was fortunate too, as he would not live to see another Assembly, dying prematurely on December 17, 1648.

Hetherington eulogized him as "one of those bright and powerful spirits which are sent in troublous times to carry forward God's work among mankind, and recalled to heaven when that work is done."[8] Hetherington also lavished this praise: "George Gillespie was one of that peculiar class of men who start like meteors into sudden splendor, shine with dazzling brilliancy, then suddenly set behind the tomb, leaving their compeers equally to admire and to deplore."

Although the youngest member of the Assembly, he led in the debates on government against some of the world's best apologists for Erastianism (Selden and Lightfoot) and Independency (Goodwin and Nye). At a strategic moment, another even more famous Scot yielded the floor to the younger Gillespie. Following Selden's learned speech,

> Samuel Rutherford turned eagerly and appealingly to young Gillespie, and said, "Rise, George, rise up, man, and defend the right of the Lord Jesus Christ to govern by his own laws the Church he has purchased with his blood." George rose, calm, steady, and confident. It was a tremendous hour and a tremendous undertaking for a young man of thirty-one to answer Selden. But the stripling knew what he had in his sling. He answered Selden so effectually, so crushingly, that the giant was silenced. He is reported to have said, "That young man has by a single speech swept away the learning and labor of ten years of my life.[9]

Surmises Beveridge, "When the Assembly met, he was little more than thirty; in five years his meteoric career had closed. In that short time his work was done, and wonderfully done. 'With the fire of youth he had the wisdom of age.' "[10]

Archibald Johnston, Lord Wariston

Archibald Johnston, who later became known as Lord Wariston, was a rising legal star in Scotland when Charles I sought to impose formality in worship and hierarchical rule in the church. A godly ruling elder with legal background, sound judgment, talent in negotiation, and commitment to religious freedom, Johnston became a leader in the reform of the Scottish church in 1638. When the General Assembly of Scotland met in 1638 in Glasgow to frame what would come to be known as the Solemn League and Covenant, Johnston was unanimously chosen to be clerk of the Assembly. At the young age of 27, this shrewd lawyer, who was "apt to forget time on his knees, a man of power with his brethren" was becoming one of the leaders in the Scottish church.

Prior to this, the king had sought to induce Johnston to favor his causes by elevating Johnston to the order of knighthood, even installing him as a judge. But even with the addition of the title, "Lord Wariston," Johnston valued faithfulness to the covenant more than the advancement that an earthly king could bring. Of him, William Hetherington said,

> His writings, his speeches, are all characterized by calmness and ease, without the slightest appearance of heat or agitation—resulting unquestionably from that aspect of character generally termed *greatness of mind;* but which would in him be more properly characterized by describing it as a rare combination of intellectual power, moral dignity, and spiritual elevation. It was the condition of a mighty mind, enjoying the peace of God which passeth understanding—a peace which the world had not given, and could not take away.[11]

Lord Wariston attended the Assembly consistently, and frequently engaged in the discussions and debates. Even the English Parliament requested him to sit among them and aid in their deliberations, although he was not, and could not become, a member of that high court.

At a crucial juncture in the Assembly in 1646, while discussing the right of the church to be free from state control, Wariston addressed the Assembly and Parliament. Let's look into the window and catch him mid-speech:

> Until King Jesus be set down on his throne with his sceptre in his hand I do not expect God's peace, and so no solid peace from men in these kingdomes; but that soveraigne truth being established a durable peace will be found to follow hereupon....Sir, this should teach us to be as tender, zealous, and carefull to assert Christ and his Church their priviledge and right, and to forewarn all least they endanger your souls....Christ lives and reigns alone over and in his Church, and will have all done therein according to his Word and will, and that he hes given no supreme headship over his Church to any pope, king, or parliament whatsoever....Christ is a king and hes a kingdome in the externall government of his church, and that he hes set doun the lawes and offices and other substantialls thereof. Wee must not now before men mince, hold up, conceal, prudentially waive anything necessary for this testimony...nor edge away an hemme of Christ's robe royal. These would seem effects of desertions, tokens of being ashamed, affrayed, or politikly diverted.[12]

When Charles II was restored to the throne, orders were issued for the seizure of Wariston among others, but he escaped and fled to the continent. While there, he fell ill and nearly died. He never fully recovered his health. In 1663 Wariston was seized in France, brought to Scotland, tried, condemned and executed. Throughout this ordeal he was so weakened by age and illness that he could scarcely stand or speak. Yet with tranquillity and confidence in his Lord, he gave his life to the cause for which he had already given his strength.

Alexander Henderson

In 1638 Alexander Henderson was moderating a Scottish Assembly, whose purpose was to abolish the Scottish episcopacy. Charles I sent a distinguished soldier, the Marquis of Hamilton, to this group to dissolve the Assembly should it call for the bishops' resignations. As Henderson and the other Scottish presbyters did just that, the Marquis paraded in, in full military dress and took a conspicuous seat up front.

With dignity and gravity Henderson asked if it was the Assembly's desire to proceed to the trial of the bishops. At this the Marquis sprang to his feet and declared that this was not the desire of his majesty, King Charles, who had sent him to prohibit any such proceedings.

Henderson calmly thanked the Marquis, assured him of their intent to obey the king as far as possible, but further reminded him that they had a higher loyalty, with their first allegiance to the universal Sovereign. As Moderator, he then repeated the question to the Assembly. The astonished Marquis warned that such would be considered revolutionary.

Henderson calmly repeated the question a third time. At this the loyal soldier rose and declared that if another word on this subject was uttered he would dissolve the meeting. Henderson, composed, sought once again to reassure the Marquis. However, at that moment the soldier declared the Assembly dissolved on the authority of the king. After charging each member to have no more to do with this, the soldier stalked out, his sabre rattling.

Calming the excited, potentially violent, throng, which was ready to pursue the Marquis, Henderson commended the Marquis for serving his sovereign faithfully; he then reminded the Assembly that they were commissioners of a greater king, and urged them to follow the example of the king's servant and representative by obeying, even to death, the words of King Jesus. The effect was magical; the bishops were brought to the bar, convicted of rebellion, and deposed. "Mr. Henderson [conducted] the ceremony of deposition amidst a solemnity and awe that would have befitted the judgment day."[13]

Alexander Henderson, a leading Scottish commissioner at the Westminster Assembly, was born in 1583. He entered St. Andrews in 1599, receiving the Master of Arts degree in 1603. Soon after, he was appointed Professor of philosophy and rhetoric at St. Andrews, where he served until 1613. At that time, he was nominated by Archbishop Gladstone to serve the parish of Leuchars. Interestingly, at that time Henderson, later to become a stalwart defender of Presbyterianism, approved of the episcopacy.

His ordination was so opposed by the parishioners that when he arrived at the Leuchars church, he found all the doors locked. He and the other ministers climbed in through the window to hold the ordination service. Later, Henderson heard the eminent preacher, Robert Bruce of Kinnaird. As the Spirit would have it, Bruce preached on John 10, where Jesus said, "I tell you the truth, the man that does not enter the sheep pen by the gate, but climbs in by some other way, is a thief and a robber." These convicting words led to Henderson's conversion, following which he re-examined the biblical basis for church government, and became a convinced Presbyterian.

A leader on the council that drew up the National Covenant, Henderson was present when 60,000 Scots gathered to adopt the Solemn League and Covenant in 1638. When the covenant was read, according to tradition, some signed with their own blood, and confirmed the covenant by oath.

In 1642, again as moderator of the Scottish Assembly, Henderson was assigned the responsibility of responding to a letter from the English Parliament as to the feasibility of a joint meeting to further Reformation teaching and practice in the three countries. Henderson proposed that they do so along the lines of the Scottish Solemn League and Covenant; to this, Parliament consented. Henderson was thus the principal author of the framework for the calling and purpose of the Westminster Assembly.

Hetherington says this about Henderson: "Henderson was by nature a king of men, and his whole bearing and language were always kingly. He was one of those great men whom God gives to elevate a nation, and work a mighty work; and whose departure leaves that age dark, feeble, and deploring." He exhibited "unremitting devotion to the cause of truth," and "in the furnace of controversy, Henderson never departed from the gentle courtesy which becomes the servant of the Lord. In the great emergencies of the conflict between truth and error he saw what ought to be done and did it. When a course of action was once determined upon, he followed it strenuously and persistently until the result was secured."[14] He ruled as Moderator with "a hand of steel in a velvet glove," and was "the destroyer in Scotland of a church government alien to the faith and spirit of the people; as the penman of the Solemn League and Covenant; as the proposer of the Westminster Assembly; as the leading commissioner of the Church of Scotland in that great body; as the friend of the kin; as the unifier of the forces of righteousness and order in the Church and State, he stands a man whose like either Church or State have seldom known."[15]

His colleague Baillie eulogized him as "that glorious soul of worthy memory, who is now crowned with the reward of his labors for God and for us...fragrant among us so long as pure and free Assemblies remain in this land, which I hope will be till the coming of the Lord."[16] Another said that Henderson "ranks next to John Knox in our Scottish history...the fairest ornament, after Mr. John Knox, of incomparable memory, that ever the Church of Scotland did enjoy."[17]

In 1898, historian William Henry Roberts assessed:

> In [America] the popular government which Henderson loved, and which finds its roots in the Calvinistic system, has come to full development. Do you ask for one monument of Henderson and his colaborers, look upon the Republic, free, united, prosperous. Do you ask for another, look upon the Presbyterian churches of this land, loyal to the core, despite all opposition, to the truth of God. May the Presbyterians of this land be as true as the fathers of the Calvinistic system.[18]

These were some of the heroes of the Assembly. Regardless of how they were chosen, it would be difficult to select better divines. Had different commissioners been present, it is unlikely that significant changes would have resulted, because these 151 participants were representative. As Beveridge allows, "it is not easy to see how the doctrinal conclusions reached by the Assembly could have been much otherwise."

Questions for Review.

1. What does Romans 5:1–5 tell us about how character is formed? Was this true in regard to these players?

2. Find a single virtue that best describes each of the characters profiled in this chapter. Can you match a Scripture verse with each one?

3. Review 2 Corinthians 3:2. How are these "living letters" useful for us today?

4. These men saw themselves as servants of King Jesus. What effect does an understanding of the kingship of Christ have on your life?

5. Compare these men with the biblical characters mentioned in Hebrews 11. What similarities/differences do you see?

For Discussion.

1. Is it wrong to have heroes? Does the Bible commend modeling our lives after spiritual leaders?

2. Optional: From your own reading, summarize the life of one other contemporary of the Assembly.

Spotlight: Simeon Ashe

Simeon Ashe, educated at Emmanuel College, Cambridge, began his preaching ministry in Staffordshire, England. Later he was chaplain to the Earl of Manchester, also serving as an army chaplain in 1642 (as did a number of others who would later serve in the Westminster Assembly). Ashe was minister at Michael Basing-Shaw in London, and later, until his death, at St. Austin's in London.

According to James Reid, "Mr. Ashe had a good estate, and a liberal heart. He was very hospitable; and his house was much frequented, and he himself was highly esteemed. He was a Christian of the primitive simplicity; and a non-conformist of the old stamp. He was eminently distinguished, by a holy life, and a cheerful mind. Holiness is the bright ornament of the Christian, the glory of angels, the beauty of heaven, and the express image of God himself, who is glorious in holiness. And persons who are most strict and holy in their lives ought to be most esteemed and honored. But such persons are too often hated, reproached, and persecuted, by the world lying in wickedness, who scoff at holiness, and thereby deride God himself. Holiness is peculiarly becoming, in the ministers of religion, who minister about holy things, and ought to be exemplary to the people."

Much of his character is revealed in the words of his fellow Westminster divine, Edmund Calamy, who eulogized Ashe as:

A man of great sincerity, humility, benevolence, prudence, and patience: as eminently diligent in preaching the glorious gospel of the grace of God in season and out of season, so as not to please the ear, but to wound the heart; seeking not the applause of men, but the salvation of souls: as singularly careful in visiting the sick: as excelling in prayer, and in maintaining great acquaintance and communion with God. His death was conformable to his life. He was rich in faith, and in other fruits of the Holy Spirit, and an eminent follower of those who through faith and patience inherit the promises. He died very comfortably, in the cheerful exercise of faith, and abounding in the consolations of the gospel of Christ, molested neither with doubts nor fears. And he was peculiarly attentive to the spiritual improvement of those who were about him. He warmly recommended Jesus Christ to them."

Mr. Calamy says,

When I was with him he took occasion to complain much, and not without just cause, that ministers, when they met together, discoursed not more of Christ, of heaven, and of the concernments of the other world; professing that if God should restore him, he would be more careful in his discourses, and more fruitful than ever he had been. He exhorted me and other ministers to preach much of Jesus Christ, and to speak of Christ to him; saying, "When I consider my best duties, I sink, I die, I despair; but when

I think of Christ, I have enough; he is all and in all. I desire to know nothing but Jesus Christ and him crucified. I account all things dung and dross, that I may be found in Christ."

Upon his death it was said that the church had lost a choice pillar and that the city of London had lost an ancient, faithful minister. He was called a "Bezaleel in God's tabernacle, a master builder, an old disciple—a burning and shining light." Samuel Rutherford spoke of him as the "gracious and zealous Mr. Ashe." Says one biographer, "Mr. Ashe, desiring to know nothing but Jesus Christ and him crucified, in this awful season, said farther: 'It is one thing to speak of Christ and of heaven, and another thing to feel the consolation of Christ and of heaven, as I do.' " One historian has gathered together a few choice sayings of Mr. Ashe, among which are: " 'Without me,' saith Christ, 'you can do nothing'; neither without him can we endure any thing. And he only can support the sinking soul under the most smarting troubles and heavy oppressions.—We may safely sail through Christ's blood into the bosom of the Father.—Truth, not words, feeds the soul: and I much rather desire, in my ministry, to profit, than to please, my auditory.—Former failings bewailed, shall not interrupt the course of future kindness."

4. God's Scriptures

All the Scriptures...the breathings of God's spirit, are
to be expected in this Garden: and those commands of
attending to the Scripture only, and to observe what
is written, is a plain demonstration that God hath tied
us to the Scriptures only: so that as the child in the
womb liveth upon nourishment conveyed by the
Navel cleaving to it, so doth the Church live only
upon Christ by the Navel of the Scripture, through
which all nourishment is conveyed.[1]

Peering through this, the clearest of windows, we can view
the very heart of the Assembly. Through this window we
can examine the principles behind our historic faith.

Note: As we get into these chapters on the themes of the
Westminster Assembly, scan a copy of the Westminster Confession of Faith (WCF). Familiarize yourself with its contents and
keep it on hand as you read these chapters. (A word about WCF
references: chapters and paragraphs are referred to by their
number designations, e.g., chapter 1, paragraph 5 is 1.5.)

All of the great Protestant confessions of the sixteenth and
seventeenth centuries recognized Holy Scripture as authoritative and unrivaled by any other source—not just superior by
degree, but in kind. Scripture issued from God, and because of
that divine origin, had no other source as its equal.

What is unique about the WCF, however, is how refined
and how explicit this base of authority is made from the outset.

In few confessions is Scripture more prominent or extensive. The esteem in which the Westminster divines held the Bible is obvious. Where most confessions would begin with a discussion of God, or faith, or other basic matters, the WCF starts by highlighting Scripture. This is not to say that the Assembly elevated the Bible over God, but only to recognize its honest attempt to communicate its basis to all who would follow.

The WCF statement about Scripture is one of the most thorough chapters in the entire confession. It is also perhaps the most extensive post-Reformation confessional statement on the subject. This first chapter became a hallmark of Presbyterianism for centuries to follow. Noted B. B. Warfield, "There is certainly in the whole mass of confessional literature no more nobly conceived or ably wrought-out statement of doctrine than [this] chapter...placed at the head of their Confession and laid at the foundation of their system of doctrine."[2] Philip Schaff has reckoned it "the best Protestant counterpart of the Roman Catholic doctrine of the rule of faith....No other Protestant symbol has such a clear, judicious, concise, and exhaustive statement of this fundamental article of Protestantism."[3]

Few who know and believe the Bible will dispute the claims of this first chapter, and it has served as a mighty fortress for many believers, especially in times of assault on Scripture.

In a sense, as we look through this window on the Westminster Christians, we could look equally into other Protestant windows of the time, and find a great chorus of believers who confessed the same thing about the Bible as did the Westminster divines.

Warfield suggests that this first chapter was in exact agreement with other summary statements of the day, in fact, likely even modeled from parts of the earlier Irish Articles of Religion (1615). However, there were also other contributors. One could compare a paragraph written by the Scotsman George Gillespie to see how similar his language is to WCF 1.5:

> The Scripture is known to be indeed the word of God by the beams of divine authority it hath in itself...such as the heavenliness of the matter; the majesty of the style; the irresistible power over the conscience; the general scope, to abase man and to exalt God; nothing driven at but God's glory and man's salvation...the supernatural mysteries revealed therein, which could never have entered the reason of men; the marvelous consent of all parts and passages (though written by divers and several penmen), even where there is some appearance of difference...these, and the like, are characters and marks which evidence the Scriptures to be the word of God.[4]

This first chapter is probably a composite, contributed by many authors, ranging from Gillespie to the Irish archbishop, James Ussher. Yet the cardinal point is to see this as an authentic expression of true Protestantism, a collaborative effort by many Bible-believers from diverse backgrounds and traditions. In short, this was a definitive statement of what the Bible is, and how it is to be viewed, not just by an individual, or a few men, but as representative of the very best of international Protestant thinking. It is the harmonious view of many believers.

Attributes of Scripture

This first paragraph of the WCF teaches that the Scriptures are necessary because humans are unable to know God unless he chooses to reveal himself.

People are unable to know those things which God has not revealed. We can only know what he has chosen to make known through Scripture (Deut. 29:29). God also reveals himself through creation. The Psalmist affirms that "the heavens declare the glory of God, the skies show his handiwork...There is no speech or language where their voice is not heard" (Ps. 19:1, 3). Romans 1:20 also testifies that the power and eternal godliness of our Lord may be known through that which is created. True knowledge is revealed by way of the created order, yet it is insufficient to lead us to ample truth. Some things may be deduced from the creation, but not enough to know Christ as our Savior.

All human beings are given enough through nature around them, so as to require them to seek this Creator. If they refuse to do this, they have enough revealed information to render them guilty before God. However, this additional information is not available from the "light of nature" or "the works of creation and providence." For additional information about salvation and godly living, we must turn to Scripture.

As one of the participants of the Assembly, Anthony Burgess, wrote: "As for that dangerous opinion, that makes God's calling of man to repentance by the Creatures, to be enough and sufficient, we reject, as that which cuts at the very root of free grace: A voice, indeed, we grant they have, but yet they make like Paul's trumpet, an uncertain sound; men cannot by...[creation]...know the nature of God and his Worship, and wherein our Justification doth consist."[5]

Assemblyman William Bridge stated, "Though Human Reason be a Beam of Divine Wisdom, yet if it be not enlightened with an higher Light of the Gospel, it cannot reach unto the things of God as it should....For though reason be the Gift of God, yet it doth proceed from God as he is God, and General Ruler of the World."[6]

By giving Scripture, God perfectly met our human desire to know more than we could learn from the natural order. The WCF lists the purposes for which God gave Scripture: (1) for the better, more sure, spreading of the truth; (2) for the sounder establishment of the church on the foundation of the unchanging Scriptures; (3) for the comfort of Christians, when they were undergoing trials associated with the weakness of the flesh or the attack of Satan; (4) for a perpetual record in writing, so as to settle disputes and give us guidance.

With these purposes in mind, God gave the Scriptures, which were "most necessary," in that God's former ways of revealing himself—through dreams, prophets, miraculous signs, and audible voice—were no longer his modes of revelation. These ceased with the age of the apostles and prophets (Eph. 2:20 and 3:5). Since then God has committed his sufficient will and mind in the canon of Holy Scripture.

The second paragraph of the WCF lists the books of the canon (which means measuring rod, or standard) of sacred Scripture. These 66 books alone are recognized as "Holy Scripture, or the Word of God written" (1.2). In addition, the WCF ascribes unique status and authority to these, "All which are given by inspiration of God, to be the rule of faith and life." No other written works were to be submitted to as "inspired," or breathed-by-God, except these. This conviction follows the teaching of Paul, written long ago: "All Scripture is God-breathed (literally, inspired), and is profitable for doctrine, reproof, correction, and training in righteousness" (2 Tim. 3:16). The WCF is only seeking to say that which Scripture itself says.

It is important to recall that this was in stark contrast to the Roman Catholic tradition of the time. Over the centuries the Roman Catholic church, when unable to sufficiently document its new dogmas, resorted to writings outside Scripture. It turned, in part, to the books known as the Apocrypha (a set of books containing fables, some history, and other writings usually to support one religious sect or other collected over the years).

Unfortunately the medieval church gave these books the same authority as Scripture, and it was left to the reformers and confessions to restore the original canon to the church. Those apocryphal books were *never* part of the original; they were added later. The apocryphal books were not inspired (2 Tim. 3:16) as were the biblical books, and hence they have no more authority in the church than any other human writings. There's a crucial difference between writings that are infallible and those that are sometimes helpful.

These fathers of the faith received the words of Scripture like the early Thessalonian disciples, who "received it as it really is, the word of God (1 Thess. 2:13). As one historian observed, amidst the first assault on the original intent of the Confession, those who seek to pervert the plain meanings of these paragraphs, must not only distort Scripture, but history itself, so abundant was the testimony of the original intent. Concludes Warfield, "If they [the divines] did not believe in these doctrines, human language is incapable of expressing belief in doctrines. Is it not a pity that men are not content with corrupting our doctrines, but must also corrupt our history?"[7]

Authority, Perfection and Clarity of Scripture

Paragraphs 4 through 7 of the first chapter state that the authoritative status of Scripture does not depend on the word of any individual, nor even collectively on the church. At the time, the standard Roman Catholic ground for the authority of the Scriptures was not "because the Bible tells me so," but "because the Church tells me so." If a church was corrupt, and the authority of Scripture depended on it, then Christians were in trouble.

Thus the WCF desired to set out the proper basis for authority—the sole, unchanging and infallible basis—God himself. The WCF says that the authority for which Scripture should be believed and obeyed depends only on God (who is truth himself) as the author. Therefore it is to be received as authoritative in all matters because it comes directly from God who cannot lie. The belief in the Scripture's authority is a by-product of our belief in God as infallibly truthful and incapable of lying. These authors tied the truthfulness of Scripture to the very character of God.

These paragraphs also tell us that, even though certain proofs of the Bible may be helpful from time to time, they will not sufficiently prove the truthfulness and authority of Scripture. Scripture is so perfect in itself, that as a person (even a non-Christian) reads it, he may be profoundly moved and even come to a "high and reverent esteem of holy Scripture." Due to the sheer heavenliness of the matters considered, the effectiveness of the things taught to change lives in this world, the literary majesty of the style, the unified consistency of all its parts (spanning over a thousand pages in most editions, without real internal contradiction), and the teaching about God's glory and our salvation, people may come to have great respect for the Bible. But respect and admiration is one thing; bowing to Scripture as one's authority for living is another. The Bible does not present itself as a book to be respected, but as a revelation to be obeyed. It does have numerous "incomparable excellencies and entire perfection," but those character traits are not the ones that lead us to submit to Scripture.

Paragraph 5 closes by stating that the person reading Scripture will not come to a full persuasion of its truth until or unless the Holy Spirit works with the Word in that person's heart.

Many Christians want so desperately to communicate the truth of the Bible to their friends or family that they fall into the trap of trying to reason someone into accepting Scripture. While we certainly should share the gospel, we must remember that the unbeliever (Rom. 2:14, 15; 8:7) will not and cannot comprehend the things of the Lord, until he is born again and made new. Our reasoning ability will not convince anyone that he should obey Scripture—that is the work of the Holy Spirit.

Assemblyman Samuel Rutherford put it well: "The preaching of the word only, if alone without the Spirit, can no more make an hair white or black, or draw us to the Son, or work repentance in sinners, than the sword of the Magistrate can work repentance....What can preaching of man or angel do without God, is it not God and God only who can open the heart?"[8]

In the middle of paragraph 6 we see this teaching continue: "Nevertheless, we acknowledge the inward illumination of the Spirit of God to be necessary for the saving understanding of such things as are revealed in the word." The Spirit convinces of authority, but the presence and work of the Holy Spirit is also necessary to illumine the Word. Apparently the authors looked to the Holy Spirit for much, and were not expecting that growth in the Word would come apart from his vital ministry.

Paragraph 6 states that God's whole counsel (Acts 20:28) regarding our salvation and life is either explicitly set forth in the Bible, or else by properly researched implications, may be learned from Scripture. Certainly there are particulars that God has not revealed to us. Often, matters have to be decided by common sense, according to the general principles revealed in God's Word.

This paragraph says that nothing at any time is to be added to Scripture, either by new revelation or by tradition. This sufficiency of Scripture is an age-old teaching, and one that protects us from innovators who think they know God better than the original writers of Scripture. As Revelation 22:18, 19 warns: "If anyone adds anything to [the words of the prophecy of this book]...God will add to him the plagues described in this book. And if anyone takes words away from this book of prophecy, God will take away from him his share in the tree of life and in the holy city, which are described in this book."

Paragraph 7 goes on to state that while some things in the

Bible are hard to understand, the basics, the things we need to know, are so clear that anyone may understand them. The Bible is not stamped "For Theologians Only." The authors of the WCF realized that some verses of Scripture are not easy to interpret. Yet the fundamentals that God wants us to know ("those things which are necessary to be known, believed, and observed for salvation") are clearly set forth. Theologians call this the perspicuity of Scripture, and G.I. Williamson has helpfully referred to this as the "see-through-ableness" of Scripture.

There is no prerequisite of higher education to understand grace. It is not by works, nor by superior intellect that Scripture works. The Bible is not intended only for the super-intelligent. It is composed, under God's inspiration, to be understood by the ordinary person.

The eighth paragraph clarifies the real basis of the biblical faith. During the Reformation there was a revival of interest in the original Greek and Hebrew texts of the Bible. Accordingly, the WCF teaches that it was the original manuscripts, the Old Testament in Hebrew and the New Testament in Greek, that were "immediately inspired…and therefore authentical." It is not a particular Bible version that is inerrant, but the earliest Greek and Hebrew texts, which have been faithfully translated in modern English versions, e.g., the NIV, NASB, NKJV. It was the original manuscripts which God kept pure and without corruption throughout all ages "by his singular care and providence."

This being the case, if we wish to settle any controversy or point of interpretation, the final appeal is to the Scriptures, not the church, nor a learned individual, although these may be aids. Accordingly, it is God's will that these original languages be translated so that the Word of God can be read in the common language of the people. It is God's desire that his revelation be known to many, and contrary to an earlier impulse which kept the Scriptures in Latin, the Westminster teaching is that the

Bible is far too valuable to be locked up only in the possession of the clergy.

God wants the Word translated so his people can have the word of God richly dwelling in them (cf. Col. 3:16), and that they may acceptably worship him, and "through patience and comfort of the Scriptures, may have hope." Thus, God wants his people to know and understand his Word.

The final two paragraphs of the first chapter go together, and targeted existing errors of the day. The ninth paragraph speaks of the unity of Scripture (that the sense of Scripture is to be interpreted with consistency, without internal contradictions), and established a rule for interpreting Scriptures. The authors of the WCF wanted the common person to have confidence that they, too, could interpret the Bible. These divines had already admitted that some passages would be difficult to interpret, and that any valid interpretation must rest on the original language version of the Bible. But in this paragraph, they confess that the way to arrive at truthful interpretations of the Bible is to compare Scripture with Scripture. This "infallible rule of interpretation" is to seek the meaning for a difficult passage in the clarity of a more straightforward verse.

For example, if we read in Romans 8:1 that "there is no *condemnation* for those who are in Christ Jesus," we may wonder what that means. It is not immediately clear whether this means that no one will ever judge us to be bad, or if this refers to God's view of the believer. If we look up other uses of the word condemnation, we see that it means, "to pronounce guilty in light of sin," and also that another verse in the same chapter uses this word. In Romans 8:33 we see that no charges against God's elect convince the Father, for it is "God who justifies" and Christ Jesus who died and was raised to life for our justification—this is the opposite of condemnation. We can now use this clarified meaning to better understand verse 1. This is how to interpret Scripture with Scripture.

The final paragraph makes clear that the Bible alone is authoritative in settling questions about religion. Prior to the Reformation, clerical councils, or "doctors" of the church, interpreted Scripture. Here, however, the WCF declares that Scripture is the "supreme judge by which all...decrees of councils, opinions of ancient writers, doctrines of men" or claims to private spiritual enlightenment are examined. When the Bible speaks, we are to examine all other thoughts by it (2 Cor. 10:5 speaks of taking every thought captive to obedience to the Word), and "we are to rest" in the teaching of Scripture. This is because the Holy Spirit speaks in the Scriptures. It is not a dead book, but rather alive, and "sharper than any double-edged sword," even able to dissect, as with a surgeon's scalpel, very closely related matters (Heb. 4:12, 13).

Jesus said that Scripture was so perfect, so interrelated that it "cannot be broken" (John 10:35). Our Lord also affirmed the Old Testament as being totally truthful; so much so, that "until heaven and earth disappear, not the slightest letter, not the least stroke of a pen, will by any means disappear" (Matt. 5:18). Paul said to Timothy that "all [not some] Scripture is God-breathed and...useful" (2 Tim. 3:16), and the apostle Peter taught that "no prophecy of Scripture came about by the prophet's own interpretation....but men spoke from God as they were carried along by the Holy Spirit" (2 Pet. 1:20, 21).

These views are mirrored in the WCF. Assemblyman Edward Reynolds wrote, "The Scriptures...are the alone rule of all controversies....So then the only light by which differences are to be decided, is the word, being a full canon of God's revealed will."[9] Samuel Rutherford was of the opinion that "the Scripture makes itself the judge and determiner of all questions and controversies in religion."[10] George Gillespie spoke of "the written word of God [as] surer than any voice which can speak in the soul of a man, and an inward testimony may sooner deceive us than the written word can; which being so, we may and ought to try the voice which speaks in the soul by the voice of the Lord which speaks in the Scripture."[11]

Turn of the century scholar B. B. Warfield, who valiantly sought to resist new attacks on the Bible, concludes of this first chapter in the WCF:

> If it be compared in its details with the teachings of Scripture, it will be found to be but the careful and well-guarded statement of what is delivered by Scripture concerning itself. If it be tested in the cold light of scientific theology, it will commend itself as a reasoned statement, remarkable for the exactness of its definitions and the close [connection] of its parts....Numerous divergences from it have been propounded of late years, even among those who profess the Westminster doctrine as their doctrine. But it has not yet been made apparent that any of these divergences can commend themselves to one who would fain hold a doctrine of Scripture which is at once Scriptural and reasonable, and a foundation upon which faith can safely build her house. In this case, the old still seems to be better.[12]

Questions for Review.

1. What is the difference between revelation from nature and special revelation? How does the WCF distinguish the two?

2. What were God's purposes in committing Scripture to writing?

3. What is the difference between the terms *inspired, infallible,* and *inerrant*? Which of these terms appear in the Bible? In the WCF?

4. Why does the WCF stress the finality of Scripture?

5. Find and discuss a few examples of Scripture interpreting other Scripture.

For Discussion.

1. How and why is the first chapter of the WCF a premier statement of Protestantism?

2. How is inerrancy tied to the character of God?

3. Why do many people think the Bible is so impossible to interpret?

Spotlight: William Gouge

William Gouge (1575–1653) was born in Middlesex County, England. He entered King's College in Cambridge in 1595 and during his nine years there was known for his attendance at 5:30 a.m. morning prayers. Gouge resolved to read 15 chapters a day from the Holy Scriptures—5 in the morning, 5 after dinner and 5 before bed. This knowledge of Scripture permeated his life, writing and ministry.

While at Cambridge, Gouge became one of the best students of the Jewish rabbi who taught Hebrew. Following his graduation he was not only an excellent Hebrew scholar, but also a lecturer in logic and philosophy in the college. In 1607 he was ordained and began his ministry at Black Friars Church (London) the following year. He often said that the pinnacle of his ambition was to go from Black Friars directly to heaven. His wish was apparently granted because he spent 46 years there, his entire ordained ministry. He is an excellent example to us of the value of a long ministry to one congregation.

Although he was well educated, his preaching was simple and clear. He said,

> Remember, we do not mount the pulpit to say fine things, or eloquent things. We have there to proclaim the good tidings of salvation to fallen men; to point out the way of eternal life; to exhort, to cheer and support the suffering sinner; these are the glorious topics upon which we have to enlarge—and will these permit the tricks of oratory, or the studied beauties of eloquence? Shall truths and counsels like these be couched in terms which the poor and ignorant cannot comprehend? Let all eloquent preachers beware lest they fill any man's ear with sounding words, when they should be feeding his soul with the bread of everlasting life!—Let them fear lest instead of honoring God, they honor themselves! If any man ascend the pulpit with the intention of uttering "A Fine Thing," he is committing a deadly sin.

Following morning worship, neighbors who were unable to attend came to his own house where he delivered his sermons again. Gouge was sensitive to keeping the Sabbath throughout his life. His own servants were not required to provide Saturday evening meals so that they might go to bed and prepare for the Lord's day. "Men," he said, "by the manner in which they 'regard this day to the Lord,' discover the real complexion of their minds relative to him. This day will declare whether they have any knowledge and fear of God, any faith, hope, and delight in him, any love to, or desire after him." Opponents mocked Gouge by calling him the "arch-Puritan."

While serving in the Westminster Assembly he was frequently called on to be moderator pro tem in the absence of the moderator, and early in October, 1644 Gouge was one of the leaders appointed to the committee to examine prospective ministers. He also was the author of the *Annotations* (in the Bible Commentary by the Westminster divines) on First Kings through the Book of Job. Two of his more important works, *Domesticall Duties* and *The Whole Armour of God*, were collected under the title *The Workes* (1627). He also wrote an influential two-volume commentary on Hebrews (1655).

Later he was chosen as President of Sion College, which was a hotbed of Puritanism. Gouge also exemplified the generosity of true piety when he supported poor scholars in the university at his own expense, as well as liberally giving to others who were impoverished.

Gouge routinely rose about 4:00 a.m. to have his own devotions, and often prayed and fasted. Of his desire to love Christ with all his soul, mind and strength, he said: "When I look upon myself, I see nothing but emptiness and weakness; but when I look upon Christ, I see nothing but fulness and sufficiency. Every thing that we need is found in Christ, and may be derived from him as the vital head of the Church....One thing we are certain of—that no being in the universe can fill his place, and do for us what he is able to do."

To his friends who came to visit him on his deathbed, he said, "I am willing to die, having, I bless God, nothing to do but to die." He called death his best friend next to Jesus Christ. His death spared him the persecution of the Great Ejection of 1662, when most Puritan leaders were forced out of their pulpits. His spiritual legacy was passed on by an assistant, William Jenkin; his minister son, Thomas Gouge; and his son-in-law Richard Roberts who married his eldest daughter, all three of which took their stand with Christ and were ejected in 1662. Gouge could well say, "As for me and my household, we will serve the Lord" (Josh. 24:15).

5. God's Sovereignty

> The cardinal principle of the alone Headship of Jesus Christ...colored all their discussions and directed them to all their conclusions. As the sovereignty of God was the formative principle in their theology, so the sovereignty of God, the Son, was the shaping principle in their system of government and worship. The key in each case was the same. When they passed from doctrine to polity, or from polity to doctrine, or from both to worship, there was no break in the harmony.[1]

There are few parts of the Confession of Faith more contested than the chapter on God's sovereignty. A careful study, however, shows that no alternative is as compatible with the whole of Scripture as is this one.

As we consider God's sovereignty let us begin with a working definition. In the seventeenth century, the notion of sovereignty was clear—it was understood better than many of us understand it today. A sovereign was one who had authoritative rule and decision-making power. Sovereignty is an absolute term; it does not have room for the idea of shared authority. A little sovereignty is like semipregnancy; either one is or one isn't. In the 1640s this doctrine was in some respects very political. Upholding the sole sovereignty of God was interpreted as an act of political subversion.

Although Arminianism, the belief that man on his own chooses God, was popular among Anglican clergy, it was not evident at the Assembly. T. Dwight Witherspoon said, "Men may play with Arminianism in times of peace, but in the great crises of spiritual conflict there is nothing but the solid bedrock of eternal sovereignty of God on which the foot can rest with any sense of security; and in times like these, churches, as well as individuals, unconsciously become Calvinists."[2]

As people who have been raised in a society that champions freedom of choice, we may find it difficult to grasp that Scripture teaches that God is our true sovereign. The question is: Does the WCF represent true biblical teaching? Let's put aside our various backgrounds and consider the Word of God first by hearing these authors' confession of it.

The Attributes of God

In the second chapter of the WCF, the foundation for God's sovereignty is laid in his attributes: he is "immutable [unchangeable]...most holy, most free, most absolute; working all things according to the counsel of his own immutable and most righteous will, for his own glory" (2.1); "in and unto himself all-sufficient, not standing in need of any creatures which he hath made, nor deriving any glory from them....the alone fountain of all being...and hath most sovereign dominion over them, to do by them, for them, or upon them, whatsoever himself pleaseth" (2.2).

To summarize, God is unchangeable and in himself has full freedom and absolute power to do whatever he finds pleasing to himself and within his own glory.

These attributes are not only the foundation, but also the ultimate reasons why God does certain things. If we correctly understand *who* God is, then we have a better grasp on *what* he does according to Scripture. Hence the WCF is wise to depict the attributes of God from the outset. If God's character is accurately described in chapter 2, then his work in chapter 3 makes sense.

Election and Predestination

"God, from all eternity, did...ordain whatsoever comes to pass" (3.1). It's easy to be put off by this bold opening statement of chapter 3. However, the purpose of this statement appears at the end of the chapter: "The doctrine of this high mystery of predestination is to be handled with special prudence and care, that men, attending the will of God revealed in his Word, and yielding obedience thereunto, may, from the certainty of their effectual vocation, be assured of their eternal election. So shall this doctrine afford matter of praise, reverence, and admiration of God; and of humility, diligence, and abundant consolation to all that sincerely obey the gospel."

The WCF makes clear that there is great value in this teaching, but that it is a "high mystery" and to be handled with "special prudence and care." The goal of this scriptural teaching is to help persons, as they consider it, to be certain of their calling and election. The apostle Peter, too, urged his hearers to "be...eager to make your calling and election sure" (2 Pet. 1:10). To do so is to obey God and seek the mind of God.

The WCF teaches that this doctrine, if properly understood, leads to a number of practical benefits, such as praise, reverence and admiration of God, as well as humility, diligence and consolation to believers. If a person does not see this teaching as beneficial, it is likely that he misunderstands the essence of the doctrine. If we have trouble with predestination, then we need to return to Scripture and understand its threefold purpose: (1) to give God the credit in salvation, (2) to demonstrate his sovereignty as Scripture teaches; and (3) to provide comfort or assurance to the believer.

The first paragraph of chapter 3 asserts that God's decree (his plan for working out salvation and other events in history) was established not by events outside him, but instead by his own will. The wording "God, from all eternity, did" is taken from Scripture, which speaks of God establishing his plan "before the creation of the world" (Matt. 25:34; Rev. 13:8; Eph. 1:4; John 17:5, 24). Hence, before creation ever occurred, before there was an external universe, God had a plan for salvation in history and it is rooted not in external events—for there were none at that time—rather it is rooted only in his own holy and wise counsel which he determined to come about freely and unchangeably.

In 3.1, the first statement gives us the positive teaching, while the second part of the paragraph contains three disclaimers: (1) God is not the one who produces sin (Jas. 1:13); (2) human beings are willful and responsible; and (3) while God is the ultimate cause, in the process of bringing his will about, he uses many other causes—secondary causes.

Opponents of the Westminster Assembly elevated free will and human ability. Their view was that God only established things from the past in keeping with what human beings would do, so as never to violate or infringe upon their will. This position is a restatement of the ancient heresy of Pelagianism which, as early as the fifth century, was condemned by the church.

The divines took pains to make sure that God's sovereignty had full sway. Their most important consideration was to prevent any restraints from being put on God's freedom. In chapter 2 the divines confessed God as being most holy and most free. Chapter 3 therefore, could be understood as an attempt to protect God's own freedom, even at the cost of restricting others'. Recall also that the writers of chapter 3 were conscious that there was a British sovereign who, from time to time, sought to usurp God's exclusive rights.

WCF 3.2 states that indeed God does decree whatever can come to pass on any supposed conditions. Moreover the basis of his plan of salvation is not that he simply foresaw it in the future, or that it would come about because of certain conditions. It is not the case that God merely peers down the tunnel of human history to see what will happen, say in the year 2000, and then stamps his approval or disapproval on what is going to happen anyway, as if that is his plan. If that were the case, then God would not be sovereign, but human beings and human history would be. Rather, these divines had a strong belief that God was in control and that human history would conform itself to God's plan and not vice versa.

This truth of God's sovereignty is taught throughout Scripture. It can be seen clearly, for example, in Romans 9 where God speaks of determining certain things even to the extent of differentiating between identical twins at birth, according to his own will (Rom. 9:11). Romans 9:18 says that "God has mercy on whom he wants to have mercy, and he hardens whom he wants to harden," thus indicating that God is sovereign. Jesus taught that not even a sparrow "will fall to the ground apart from the will of your Father. And even the very hairs of your head are all numbered" (Matt. 10:29, 30). In Acts, the Christians, in prayer, acknowledge that God's hand determined Jesus' own death (Acts 4:28). Elsewhere in Acts it is affirmed that God foreordained or pre-ordered certain events (see, for example, Acts 2:23; 3:18–20; 13:48; 17:26).

WCF 3.3 states that God, for the manifestation of his own glory, predestined some men and angels to life; others he foreordained to everlasting death. It is crucial to see that both men and angels are included in this summary statement; thus, even the Fall and the fallen angels come under God's decree of predestination.

The careful reader will notice a word change in paragraph 3.3; i.e., that "some men and angels are *predestined* unto…life;

and others *foreordained* to everlasting death." There is a slight difference in how these words are used in Scripture (but not whether or not God has the final determination) and this wording reflects the Assembly's desire to be as close to scriptural language as possible.

These men and angels, paragraph 4 goes on to tell us, are so designed that their number cannot be increased or decreased. The thrust of this statement is not so much that an individual has absolutely no chance of entering the Kingdom of Heaven, but rather to assure us that God is truly sovereign as he says, and that our eternal destiny rests in his hand so much so, that the end result is unchangeable even by our own acts or by historical accidents. God's work of predestination and salvation is perfect, and he executes and completes it with all the perfection of who he is and in keeping with the beginning of his decree.

Imagine walking across the courtyard to peer into another window, a window that allows us to listen to the debate of those who oppose the Westminster Assembly. They take strong exception to chapter 3 in the WCF. They argue that those who end up in heaven or hell do so based on their own determination or their own freely chosen acts. They insist that the free will of human beings, rather than the sovereignty of God, determines salvation. However, as modern as these opponents sound, and as emphatic as they are on human rights and ability, when we compare their ideas to Scripture, we find that in all cases the sovereign will of God is more important and more elevated than the choice and free will of humans. The WCF authors valued God's will, ability and freedom over man's. It is important to note that none are saved by God's eternal predestination because of their own goodness, nor should they have a haughtiness as if they have some ability that others don't. In fact the Synod of Dordt states clearly that when Christ chose a certain number of human beings he did not do so because they were "better, more worthy than others, but lying in the common misery with others."

In paragraphs 5–7, the principles enumerated in paragraphs 1–4 are applied to two different classes of people: believers and unbelievers. Paragraph 5 speaks only of believers—those who, before the creation of the world, out of the mass of humanity, have been chosen by God in Christ to everlasting glory. This is taught plainly in Scripture: "For he chose us in him before the creation of the world to be holy and blameless in his sight. In love he predestined us to be adopted as his sons" (Eph. 1:4, 5). This predestination was formed in love, not in hatred nor with a petty motivation of excluding others. Moreover, Ephesians 1:3–14 begins with: "Praise be to…God" for doing this, while verse 6 praises God for his glorious grace, through which he has freely chosen us. The mystery of this choosing according to his good pleasure again leads us to be "for the praise of his glory" (Eph. 1:12).

Christians have been chosen out of God's free grace and love, and not according to nor depending on some pre-knowledge of God as to their merits. Believers are totally undeserving of his grace, period (cf. Rom. 9). The WCF has its eye toward inducing humility.

The sixth paragraph tells us that as God has appointed the elect unto eternal glory, so has he ordained the means by which this happens. The "means" are the events that lead a person to trust in God, e.g., the witness of believers, a book that stimulates spiritual interest, tragic circumstances. All of these are secondary causes, or means ordained unto the end.

In addition, this paragraph teaches that all the elect, once they are redeemed, are also called, justified, adopted and sanctified (see Rom. 8:29-32). The redemption of the elect is an act of free grace, as is their justification, adoption and sanctification. And according to this paragraph (and according to Scripture) no one but the elect is justified, adopted and sanctified.

The seventh paragraph treats the painful and controversial subject of why unbelievers are not in heaven or what happens to them. The WCF says that the rest of mankind (other than God's elect) God passes over and ordains to dishonor and wrath for their sin, which also is to the praise of his glorious justice. Again the basis for this is found within God's sovereign power over his creatures and his own good pleasure.

As to whether or not these teachings are scriptural, consider the words of the great Baptist preacher Charles Spurgeon, spoken in a sermon on 2 Thessalonians 2:13, 14: "I love to proclaim these strong old doctrines, that are called by a nickname Calvinism, but which are surely and verily the revealed truth of God as it is in Christ Jesus."

He continues, "By this truth I make a pilgrimage into the past, and as I go, I see father after father, confessor after confessor, martyr after martyr, standing up to shake hands with those who agree with the doctrine of predestination and against the doctrine of free-will."

Spurgeon reviews church history to see if he can find one great leader who stood up for the primacy of free-will and says, "I should have to walk for centuries all alone. Here and there a heretic, of no very honorable character, might rise up and call me brother. But taking these things to be the standard of my faith, I see the land of the ancients peopled with my brethren; I behold multitudes who confess the same as I do, and acknowledge that this is the religion of God's own church."

He concludes, "First, I think election, to a saint, is one of the most stripping doctrines in all the world—to take away all trust in the flesh, or all reliance upon any thing except Jesus Christ....Friends, if you want to be humbled, study election, for it will make you humble under the influence of God's Spirit. He who is proud of his election is not elect; and he who is humbled under a sense of it may believe that he is. He has every reason to believe that he is, for it is one of the most blessed effects of election, that it helps us to humble ourselves before God. Once again election and the Christian should make him very fearless and very bold. No man will be so bold as he who believes he is elect of God. What cares he for man, if he is chosen of his maker? What will he care for the pitiful chirpings of some tiny sparrows when he knows that he is an eagle of the royal race? Will he care when the beggar pointeth at him, when the blood royal of heaven runs in his veins? Will he fear if all the world stand against him? If earth be all in arms abroad, he dwells in perfect peace."

Spurgeon and many others throughout history agreed with what was rediscovered by the Reformers, and clearly stated in the Irish Confession (1615), the Synod of Dordt (1618-1619), and climatically in the Westminster Assembly in the 1640s. The teaching of Scripture is clearly set out in these doctrines. It is helpful to recall the vow taken by the members of the Westminster Assembly to remember that they were not seeking to innovate doctrine, but only to repeat that which was in Scripture" (see chapter 1 of this book).

Of the importance of this teaching, the twentieth century theologian John Murray noted:

On this crucial issue…Calvin, Dordt, and Westminster are at one. The terms of expression differ…and the Westminster Confession with inimitable finesse and brevity has given to it the most classic formulation. But the doctrine is the same and this fact demonstrates the undissenting unity of thought on a tenet of faith that is a distinguishing mark of our Reformed heritage and without which the witness to the sovereignty of God and to his revealed counsel suffers eclipse at the point where it must jealously be maintained. For the glory of God is the issue at stake.[3]

Human Responsibility

What is the proper role of human responsibility? Scripture certainly teaches that we are responsible for our actions and that Christians (and even unbelievers) take actions based on their own will. Moreover, there are statements in the Bible that seem to indicate that any person may come to God, or that "whosoever will may come." It is important as we interpret those Scriptures to neither minimize the truthfulness of those, nor to fail to harmonize those with the rest of Scripture.

What may help is to see that the Bible has statements from different viewpoints. At times we are given the divine perspective, and at other times the human perspective. The perspectives have different origins, but are in no way contradictory. So, Scripture teaches *both* that God has a sovereign will and that people have a human and reasonable responsibility. The important thing is to understand that both Old and New Testaments affirm and praise God's sovereignty as a glorious doctrine. It is not one that is hidden, nor is it a source of embarrassment to the church. The WCF authors recognized this and saw that predestination was a grand attempt to be God-centered instead of man-centered. They wanted to defend God (who lovingly executed predestination) as taking the initiative in our salvation. God was never out of control—he never needed to resort to Plan B. God's sovereignty was never thwarted. In comparison or contrast to the earthly king's authority, which could be thwarted and could be fallible, God's sovereign rule was infallible, unchangeable and irresistible.

The wording of the WCF was not chosen casually. Every phrase went through several layers of committee deliberations. After the wording was drafted, an expert committee of theologians (consisting of seven divines along with the four Scottish commissioners) refined the work, and with closer scrutiny examined the teaching before presenting this back to the Assembly as a whole. Then with one of the other major committees finally re-examining the language, it was presented to the Assembly as a whole for consideration.

Warfield says that this particular topic was discussed in excess of 20 times, even though most of the work was originated and thoroughly critiqued in committee. This can certify to us that "it was not passed by the Assembly without the most careful scrutiny or without many adjustments and alterations, so that as passed it represents clearly the deliberate and reasoned judgment of the Assembly as a whole."[4] In addition, Baillie commented on the thoroughness of the debate on this topic: "We had long and tough debates about the decrees of election; yet thanks to God that all has gone right according to our mind."[5] Warfield says,

> We have here no hasty draft, rushed through the body at breakneck speed and adopted at the end on the credit of the Committee that had drafted it. The third chapter…is distinctly the work of the Assembly itself, and comes to us as the well-pondered and thoroughly adjusted expression of the living belief of that whole body. The differences that existed between the members were not smoothed over in ambiguous language. They were fully ventilated. Room was made for them when they were considered important….We cannot say that this or that clause represents this or that party in the Assembly. There were parties in the Assembly, and they were all fully heard and what they said was carefully weighed. But no merely party opinion was allowed a place in the document. When it came to voting the statements there to be set down, the Assembly as such spoke; and in speaking it showed itself capable of speaking its own mind. It is doing only mere justice to it, therefore, to read the document as the solemn and carefully framed expression of its reasoned faith.[6]

In conclusion, if one compares the WCF with Scripture, then one will see that the Assembly authors sought to express that which was the essence of Christianity. As one historian said, the divines "conceived that their business was not to adjust the Bible to man, nor to cut and clip the Book to fit human prejudice and accommodate human conceit, but to faithfully adjust man to the Bible."[7]

Questions for Review.

1. What Scriptures teach that God has elected some from before the foundation of the world?

2. What is the difference between predestination, election and foreordination?

3. (a) In Revelation 13:8 who are *"all* whose names have not been written in the Book of Life belonging to the Lamb that was slain *before* the foundation of the world"? (cf. also Eph. 1:4, 5 and 1 Pet. 1:19, 20 to this choosing in eternity past)

   (b) Who are "certain men whose condemnation was marked out long ago" (Jude 4)? Do Ephesians 1:4 and 1 Thessalonians 1:4 teach that God elected these believers to salvation before they ever made a choice? What about the disobedient in 1 Peter 2:8? Does 2 Timothy 1:9 allow us to assert that God saves because he knows how we'll be?

   (c) Does Proverbs 16:4 mean that God even made the evil for his own purposes? Did God prepare Hell for the devil (Matt. 25:41)?

   (d) In John 17:6, 9, 12 is Jesus speaking of a definite group of those given to him by God?

4. How do you interpret Romans 9:18, 22, 23?

5. Was Jesus' death predestined? Who were "secondary causes" leading up to his death?

For Discussion.

1. Why do you think that so many people disagree with the Reformed teaching on predestination?

2. Evaluate Spurgeon's comments. Do you agree?

3. In a sentence or two, give a description of Arminianism and Pelagianism.

Spotlight: Lazarus Seaman

Born in Leicester, England and educated at Emmanuel College, Cambridge, Lazarus Seaman came to school penniless and had to drop out temporarily to teach in order to make his living. He was self-taught and served as Chaplain to the Earl of Northumberland. In 1642 he was ordained and served as Pastor of Allhallows in London. Of him a contemporary said, "He was a person of a most deep, piercing, and eagle-eyed judgment in all points of controversial divinity. He had few equals, if any superiors, in ability to decide and determine a dark and doubtful controversy. He could state a theological question with admirable clearness and acuteness, and knew how, in a controversy, to cleave, as we say, a hair. Nor was he less able to defend than to find out the truth."

He was so respected in debate that sometimes his opponents were disheartened upon seeing his name on the list of speakers. In 1644 he became Master of Peterhouse College at Cambridge and took a public declaration of his desire to see the University reformed: "I do solemnly and seriously promise, in the presence of Almighty God, the Searcher of all hearts, that, during the time of my continuance in that charge, I shall faithfully labor to promote piety and learning in myself, the fellows, scholars, and students, who do or shall belong to the said College, agreeably to the late solemn national league and covenant…and by all means to procure the welfare, and perfect reformation both of that College and University, so far as to me appertains."

He was known for his debating skill and his excellence as an expositor of Scripture. He was ejected in the Act of Uniformity in 1662. A contemporary said of him, "I never admired his scholarship so much as I did his patience, the lesson in which he grew so perfect in the School of affliction….Dr. Seaman was a burning and shining light…a scribe instructed to the kingdom of heaven, like a man who is an householder, who bringeth out of his treasure things new and old. I may justly say of him, that he was an ocean of Theology, and that he had so thoroughly digested the whole body of divinity, that he could upon all occasions discourse upon any point without labor. He was a living body of Divinity, and his tongue as the pen of a ready writer. He was a person of great stability and steadiness in the truth. I am confident that he valued one truth of Christ, above all the wealth of both the Indies.—He was deeply and tenderly sensible of the state of the church of Christ. He was ever very inquisitive how it fared with the people of God in foreign parts; and this not out of Athenian curiosity, but out of a public spirit of Christianity….Industrious and indefatigable in his Calling— Admirably prudent both in his speech and behavior—And an example of patience in suffering affliction."

6. God's Salvation

"Take away theology and give us some nice religion"
has been a popular slogan for so long that we are
likely to accept it, without inquiring whether religion
without theology has any meaning. And however
unpopular I may make myself, I shall and will affirm
that the reason why the churches are discredited
today is not that they are too bigoted about theology,
but that they have run away from theology.[1]

One of the most contested areas of Christianity prior to the
time of the Westminster Assembly was the manner in
which God saved people. The single largest source of confusion
was the teaching on the subject that had evolved in the Roman
church. One key to grasping the divines' statements on salvation is to see that they were careful to draw out these themes in
contrast to Rome's teaching of the day.

Let's gather to look through another window on
Westminster into a dimly lit room where a committee of about
25 men are working. They are dressed in their short day cloaks
rather than their long black Geneva academic gowns. Those
present have studied, preached, explained and defended biblical teaching on God's plan of salvation for years. The challenge
before them is to distill what the Bible teaches on the topics
central to salvation.

Interestingly, chapters 8–18 of the WCF, the sections most
directly concerned with God's manner of saving his people,
were some of the least controversial, and consequently least

discussed subjects before the Assembly. In contrast to the more controversial sections on God's decrees, and the lengthier chapter on Scripture (chapter 1), these portions ignited few heated debates. Basically, this is one area where the divines agreed with one another and where Scripture spoke plainly.

They understood that God's entire work of salvation was attributable to the "voluntary condescension on God's part" (7.1), which was expressed by way of the covenant. The divines were keenly aware that human beings could never bridge the gulf that separated them from God. Hence, God had to take the initiative in salvation. Had he not, there would be no salvation. This is fundamental to the Westminster view of salvation—if God had not acted first, we would not have acted at all.

The manner of God's saving is inseparable from the person and work of Jesus Christ. The Lord Jesus, the Second Person of the eternal Trinity, in accord with God's eternal purpose, voluntarily (8.4) kept the law perfectly and fulfilled for us all that Adam did not (Rom. 5:12–19). He was sinless, perfect (Heb. 4:15), and fully satisfied the Father's justice, purchasing "not only reconciliation, but an everlasting inheritance in the kingdom of heaven, for all those whom the Father had given him" (John 17:4, 6, 9, 12, 15; WCF 8.5). His substitutionary death on the cross gained salvation for us. The writers of the WCF desired to make it plain that to all those for whom Christ had purchased redemption, he also certainly and effectually applies that redemption, while also making intercession for them (Heb. 8:2); reveals the mysteries of salvation to them, working in a manner that persuades them to believe; and overcomes all their foes by his power and wisdom. All of this is done by Christ in a manner which is most compatible with his wonderful and unsearchable plan of working (Rom. 11:33–35).

The divines' consistently tie together the precious work of salvation with the earlier teachings on God's sovereignty and election. In keeping with those earlier biblical truths, they seek to portray a salvation based on the work and power of God, and not on the work and power of humans, the church or experience. In contrast to the Roman teaching that salvation came through the church, and in contrast to Protestant extremists' teaching that salvation came from elevated mystical experience, and in contrast to the newfound faith of their day, which stressed that humans worked salvation out as a by-product of their own free and rational choices, the divines presented to the church a superb declaration which stressed that salvation was of the Lord (Jon. 2:9).

This emphasis counteracts our tendency to think that there is something we can do on our own to earn God's approval—works-righteousness. This attitude cheapens grace—it is no longer amazing. If we do not clearly communicate and practice a faith that depends on God from first to last (Rom. 1:17), we diminish the gracious manner of God's salvation. It is not due to our works (Rom. 9:16), nor our efforts that we have God's salvation; it is his gift (Eph. 2:8; Rom. 4:1–8). The mid-twentieth century preacher, Donald Barnhouse, agreed with the divines when he said that all who allow for any contribution from man in salvation may as well pervert the gospel chorus "Jesus Paid It All" into:

> Jesus paid 90 percent,
> Ten percent to him I owe;
> Sin lost most of its stain,
> He washed it pink again.

In WCF chapters 10 through 18, one biblical step in salvation is discussed at a time. The authors were familiar with other Reformed statements on these subjects; moreover, these Christians had a better and more comprehensive grasp than most modern Christians. These forefathers, writing 350 years ago, evidenced a great appreciation for the wholeness and connectedness of God's salvation. Since it is his salvation, given to his people, it should be communicated as he lays it out in Scripture.

One of the frequently ignored aspects of biblical teaching is that the various parts of God's salvation are related to one another. That is to say, that when God saves a person, he not only forgives and redeems, but also freely justifies, sanctifies, adopts, and keeps until the end.

Pattern of Salvation

Scripture teaches this "order of salvation," as it is called. New Christians are encouraged to memorize John 1:12. Here they are assured that if they receive Christ and believe on his name, they will have the right to become children of God. The public process is *receive-believe-become*. However, verse 13 explains that before we can do any of those things, something invisible must happen—we must be born again. This new birth is not the result of some decision or will of a human father. God's children are "born of God." Rebirth comes before we receive and believe. In fact, we will neither receive or believe, until we are born again.

In John 3, Jesus says, "No one can see the kingdom of God unless he is born again.…No one can enter the Kingdom of God unless he is born of water and the Spirit" (John 3:3, 5). Thus, being born again precedes any spiritual insight or inheritance of eternal life. Rebirth (regeneration) must come first.

Romans 10:13 promises that "everyone who calls on the name of the Lord will be saved." However, as this Scripture passage continues, we learn that belief comes before confession (10:14), and that belief can only follow hearing the good news. People will not hear the call without the preaching of God's Word, and the preachers of God's Word must be commissioned (10:15) to go and bear the good news. The chain in this passage is that the Church sends preachers, who preach the Word so that people can hear the message. After hearing the message, those who are God's people will believe, and then will confess the Lord. And assuredly, all who call on the Lord will be saved. This is the order of salvation in Romans 10.

Perhaps one of the clearest places where the order of salvation is explained is Romans 8:28–32. Romans 8:28, that treasured verse, especially in times of trouble, does not apply to everyone, but specifically to the domain of God's people who are "called according to his purpose." The first step in this revealed order is God's purpose (or decree). Then and only then does it move to those who are called. This passage goes on to show that those who have been called according to God's purpose are also then the objects of his predestination, his calling, his justifying, and his glorifying (8:30). Thus, God, beginning with his purpose (decree) predestines, calls, justifies and keeps; so that all who are in the midst of this process can know that all things will work together for good.

To see the interconnectedness of Christian experience, one also could study Romans 5:3–5 and 2 Peter 1:5–9. In these passages, growth in grace, or the maturation of Christian virtues, are heaped upon one another as God works in our lives. Apparent in Scripture is a basic pattern, in which God takes us from death to life, from unbelief to trust, and this "so great salvation" (Heb. 2:3) is a package deal, which flowers into many different aspects, and into eternity.

Assuming the great teachings already laid out on God's decrees (WCF chapter 3), the covenant (chapter 7), and Christ (chapter 8), the WCF teaching on the order of God's salvation begins with "effectual calling" (chapter 10). Effectual (or in other places "efficacy") means that something truly takes effect in reality. It works. It is the opposite of theoretical. Effectual calling is that calling by God to forsake our sins and come to him, which really takes effect. As Jesus taught in Matthew 22:14, "Many are invited [outwardly, and not really taking effect], but few are chosen [only those effectually called]." While many outwardly hear the gospel message, only some respond. Those who respond are the ones whom God calls effectually.

Frequently Scripture speaks of God's calling (e.g., Rom. 1:1; 2 Pet. 1:10). A number of Bible commentators have observed that in the NT Epistles, the word "called" is only used of true Christians, who have been effectively drawn to God. The WCF is quick to remind us that this calling, just like our whole salvation, is due neither to our efforts nor to our response to God. It is not we who save, but God. Chapter 10 tells us that this effective call is from "God's free and special grace alone, not from anything at all foreseen in man, who is altogether passive therein, until, being quickened [see Eph. 2:4, 5] and renewed by the Holy Spirit, he is thereby enabled to answer this call, and to embrace the grace offered" (10.2).

Ephesians 2:1–10 incorporates nearly all of the individual steps of salvation. Verses 1–3 indicate that before we come to Christ, we are "dead in...transgressions and sins" (vs. 1), followers of the "ruler of the kingdom of the air, the spirit who is now at work in those who are disobedient" (vs. 2), intent on "gratifying the cravings of our sinful nature," and "by nature, objects of wrath" (vs. 3).

Into this sin-dominated life comes God's rich mercy (vs. 4). Prior to our seeing the kingdom of God (John 3:3, 5), God who is rich in mercy makes us "alive with Christ even when we were dead in transgressions—it is by grace you have been saved" (Eph. 2:5). So, God's work comes before our conscious faith. We are reborn, or "made alive with Christ"; then we can respond in faith, following rebirth. After this rebirth, the outworking of this salvation continues into the "coming ages" so that Christians can live lives that "show the incomparable riches of his grace" (vs. 7).

Verses 8–10 inform us that grace is foundational, i.e., that this grace which comes from God generates even our faith and is "not from yourselves, it is the gift of God—not by works, so that no one can boast" (vss. 8, 9). The entire work is begun and effected by the mighty grace of God. This work does not end with our salvation; it extends to our living out a Christian life as "God's workmanship, created in Christ Jesus to do good works, which God prepared in advance for us to do" (vs. 10).

Chapter 10 of the WCF notes that it is only those whom God has predestined to life that he effectually calls. Isn't this what Romans 8:28–32 teaches? Those and only those whom he effectively calls out of their state of sin and death have their minds enlightened so as to "savingly…understand the things of God, taking away their heart of stone, and giving unto them a heart of flesh; renewing their wills, and, by his almighty power, determining them to that which is good" (WCF 10.1). This is God's effective calling, a beginning step in our conversion. In this strong and sovereign act of God, Christians still come to him "most freely, being made willing by his grace" (10.1). God determines and calls; and he also makes us willing to come freely. There is no contradiction, and the authors of the WCF knew this.

The next step in God's salvation is justification. It is often taught that this means to be seen by God "just as if I'd" never sinned. Such a simple definition is helpful as it stresses that justification is an act that God alone does. We have no part in our justification. It is a legal pronouncement, with God acting as judge. To be justified is to be pronounced free from the penalty of sin, which we truly deserve.

The WCF has a superbly crafted explanation of justification, which was the same in most respects for the saved of God in both the Old and New Testaments (11.6). This justification is not rooted in persons but, in keeping with earlier teachings, "God did, from all eternity, decree to justify all the elect" (11.4). When Jesus died on the cross, he fully discharged "the debt of all those that are thus justified, and did make a proper, real, and full satisfaction to his Father's justice in their behalf.…not for anything in them; [but]…only of free grace" (11.3). To see just how biblical this statement is, one could consult the following

Scripture verses:

- Acts 13:38, 39—Christians are justified based on the forgiveness that comes only through Jesus;
- Romans 3:24—we are justified by grace, based on "the redemption that came by Christ Jesus";
- Romans 3:25, 26—God demonstrates his justice through justification, in that he is the one who justifies, in light of his punishing Christ in our place;
- Romans 5:1—we are justified through a non-works instrument, faith;
- Romans 8:1—the opposite of condemnation, justification, is our's in Christ;
- Romans 8:33–39—since it is God who justifies, no one can separate the believer from his Lord.

As we look into this window on Westminster we see deep biblical conviction. The Assembly took care to stress that faith rests on Christ alone as the instrument of justification (Gal. 3:10–12), and that true belief unites faith and work in biblical balance. If one revisits Ephesians 2:10, it is clear how God works all of grace, which if rightly understood, leads to a life of obedience.

The WCF makes it clear that justification does not somehow infuse righteousness into the believer (the Roman Catholic view) as if righteousness were pumped at a filling station, but instead, that justification is God's pardoning of our sins, as he accounts us as righteous. He does this for the sake of Christ alone, in that Jesus and the Father covenanted for a group of people before the creation of the world. On the last night of Jesus' life on earth, he presented God with the claim to redeem "all that you have given me" (John 17:4, 6, 9). We are justified only by the good pleasure of the Father, who is satisfied with Christ's obedience on our behalf. All of this, including believing, is the gift of God (11.1).

And the work of God in our lives does not end with

justification. Chapter 12 of the WCF goes on to speak of the biblical teaching of adoption. After a Christian is effectively called and justified, he is also adopted. God does not just legally save us; he also incorporates us into his very own family. Psalm 68:6 tells us that God "sets the lonely in families." In this case, God puts us into his very own family.

The Westminster divines knew that all who are justified are also adopted and given the liberties and privileges of the children of God; have his name put upon them; receive the spirit of sonship (Rom. 8:15–17); have access to the throne of grace (Heb. 4:14–16; Rom. 5:1, 2) with boldness; are enabled to cry, "*Abba*, Father" (Gal. 4:6; Rom. 8:15); are "pitied, protected, provided for, and chastened by him [Heb. 12:5–8], as by a Father; yet never cast off…and inherit the promises, as heirs of everlasting salvation" (WCF 12.1). These authors were not writing arid theological propositions. They knew the comfort of the teaching of adoption and wanted their flocks to know it too.

Anyone who has adopted a child knows that the adopted one is loved as any other child is. An adopted child is not a second-class child. Scripture teaches that each Christian is adopted into the family of God, and given stupendous privileges. The Westminster divines elevated this teaching and realized its vital importance.

Following adoption comes sanctification, the work of being made holy. Sanctification affects all parts of the redeemed person, yet is not complete in this life (13.2). The WCF reflects Paul's teaching in Romans 7, that all Christians are at times besieged by sinful impulses. And at times we cannot fathom why we do the very things we don't want to do, and fail to do those things which we know we ought to do. We will sin, and to deny that is to contradict Scripture and deceive ourselves (1 John 1:8). The Assembly was realistic enough to warn of a "continual and irreconcilable war, the flesh lusting against the Spirit, and the Spirit against the flesh" (13.2).

Sanctification applies only to those who have been effectively called, regenerated, and given a new heart (2 Cor. 5:17). These Christians are further sanctified by his [Christ's] Word and Spirit dwelling in them" (WCF 13.1), and there is gradual Christian growth. This captures the clear scriptural teaching that each person who is born again is also filled with the Holy Spirit. There are, and should be, lifelong seasons of renewal and deepening; however, Christians receive the Holy Spirit in connection with salvation, and not as a later blessing. Sanctification is part of the package deal.

These authors wrote what the Bible teaches. All who have been baptized into Christ have been baptized into his death and resurrection (Rom. 6:3, 4). This spiritual baptism refers to each Christian. Furthermore, no one can confess Jesus as Lord, without the Holy Spirit (1 Cor. 12:3) first renewing their mind. First comes renewal, then confession, as the order of salvation. Likewise, first comes calling, justification and adoption. To all those who have those graces, sanctification comes as well. God justifies no one, whom he does not also sanctify.

The next topic which the WCF takes up is saving faith (chapter 14). We do not cooperate with God in our effective call, justification or adoption. These are totally and exclusively his works. The WCF places the individual aspects of salvation in order, beginning with those steps which God alone does, and then moves into the realm in which we are conscious and cooperative. Sanctification is performed by God, but in a sense requires our cooperation (e.g., Gal. 5:25).

After we have been called, justified and adopted by God, and the process of sanctification has began, then we are called (and now able) to exercise saving faith. Chapter 14 gives an excellent, practical definition of saving faith. Saving faith is not merely acknowledging that Scripture is true—even demons do that (Jas. 2:19). It is one that believes to be true whatever "is revealed in the Word, for [as] the authority of God himself speaking therein; and acteth differently upon that which each particular passage…containeth; yielding obedience to the commands, trembling at the threatenings, and embracing the promises of God for this life, and that which is to come" (14.2). Saving faith touches the realm of behavior, and we "act differently," "tremble at threatenings," and honor the Word of God. It is the kind of faith, given to all the elect, in which they are "enabled to believe…the work of the Spirit of Christ in their hearts" (14.1). To all whom the Father calls, justifies, adopts and sanctifies, he also gives saving faith which "is increased and strengthened" (14.1) and "gets the victory" (14.3).

To whom God gives the above, he also grants repentance. Repentance is a true hatred of the "filthiness and odiousness of sin, as contrary to the holy nature, and righteous law of God" (15.2) in which redeemed persons are so grieved that they turn away from sin. The biblical word for repentance refers to an about-face, a reversal of direction, a turning away. Every Christian is to repent not only at conversion, but also afterward, and, in fact, is to "repent of…particular sins" (15.5). The divines also wanted it clearly understood that repentance is not a satisfaction for sin, nor an assistance to grant us pardon (15.3).

WCF chapters 15 ("Of Repentance") and 16 ("Of Good Works") are best understood in opposition to the Roman Catholic tradition. The divines wanted to make sure that their sheep were not in bondage to the system, which taught that penitence was a sacrament, or that a person could accumulate good works to earn God's favor.

We've already seen in Ephesians 2:10 that he who is born again is expected to grow in doing good. Jesus taught that those who belonged to him would do the works of the Father (Matt. 7:21–23). God expects us, once born again and filled with the Spirit, to serve and obey him (16.1). But works are never the basis for salvation or sanctification.

The final two chapters in this section involve the perseverance of the saints and assurance of salvation. We have already seen in Romans 8:32 that not only does God call, decree, predestine and justify, but moreover, that those who are the objects of this grace are also glorified. This refers to the final state, when even our bodies will no longer show any defects of sin. This act of God, which he has freely given us in the One he loves, is given to all "whom God hath accepted in his Beloved [Eph. 1:6], effectually called, and sanctified by his Spirit" (17.1). It assures that such people "can neither totally nor finally fall away from the state of grace, but shall certainly persevere therein to the end, and be eternally saved" (17.1).

Whether we call this "eternal security," or "once saved, always saved," or the "preservation of the saints," it is still a thoroughly biblical teaching. In John 10:27–29, Jesus says, "My sheep listen to my voice; I know them, and they follow me. I give them eternal life, and they shall never perish; no one can snatch them out of my hand...no one can snatch then out of my Father's hand." Earlier, our Lord had taught that if we feed on him, he will keep us until the last day and raise us up (John 6:54). Paul assures the Christians at Phillipi that when God begins a good work (of salvation) in people, he will continue it until its completion (Phil. 1:6). Peter speaks of an "inheritance that can never perish, spoil or fade—kept in heaven for you who through faith are shielded by God's power" (1 Pet. 1:4, 5).

Once we're born again, there is no later change in our nature (John 3:1–8). And since Christ's death was once and for all (Heb. 9:25–28), in that all who are Christians have died with him (Rom. 6:4–8), we die to sin once, and from then on are irrevocably members of God's family. We are given the utmost assurance of this when Romans 8 tells us that nothing, "neither death nor life, neither angels nor demons, neither the present nor future, nor any powers, neither height nor depth, nor anything else in all creation, will be able to separate us from the love of God that is in Christ Jesus our Lord" (Rom. 8:38, 39).

Those in whom God begins his work of salvation—those who are called, justified and elected—will also stay with God until the end, to glorification (Rom. 8:30).

Although God gives perseverance, the WCF is astute enough to warn us that there will be rough times (17.3). Still however, we receive great comfort from the basis of this perseverance. This author has used WCF 17.2 repeatedly in counseling sessions with tenderhearted Christians, to encourage them to recognize the true basis of their faith: not in themselves, but God. The Assembly divines knew the value of this as well, for they taught that our perseverance, far from depending on us, depended on:

- the immutability (unchangeableness) of the decree of election (Rev. 13:8);
- the free and unchangeable love of God the Father (Eph. 1:4, 5; Rom. 8:39);
- the effectiveness of the merit and intercession of Jesus Christ (Heb. 7:25; Rom. 5:8);
- the indwelling spirit (John 15),
- the seed of God planted within them (1 John 3:9);
- the nature of the covenant of grace (Heb. 6:17, 18).

Such perseverance is a gift of God, and delivers us from worrying that God, like many fickle human lovers, might one day fail to be our saving spouse. The more we know the salvation of our God, the more clearly we see that he will be faithful to the end, that he will not disown himself (2 Tim. 2:13), and that we can be assured that "if we died with him, we will also live with him; if we endure, we will also reign with him" (2 Tim. 2:11, 12).

The final chapter in this section on God's salvation is on assurance. Although there may be times or seasons in our life when this assurance is shaken, at low levels, or besieged (WCF 18.4), still it will not totally be quenched. This assurance is not based on conjecture nor probability (18.2). It is rather based on: the divine promises of salvation (Gal. 3:18); the inward evidence of those graces (Gal. 5:22–26); the testimony of the Spirit of adoption confirming that we are God's children (Rom. 8:15–17); and the indwelling Holy Spirit, who is the deposit of our inheritance (Eph. 1:13, 14).

The WCF recognizes that this assurance is sometimes counterfeited (Heb. 6:4–6) by hypocrites and presumptuous people, but that all who truly believe in the Lord will have some measure of this assurance. God does not want his children to wonder perpetually whether or not they are accepted in the beloved. Once we are saved, God's Spirit also assures us of God's faithfulness to keep us. Toward the end of his life, the apostle John believed that we could know that our salvation was certain. In 1 John 5:13 he says that he writes these truths so that we may *know* (not guess) that we have eternal life.

God's salvation is generous, it extols his sovereign power, and it is by grace from first to last. The composer J. S. Bach shared these views and signed his compositions *soli deo gloria*, to God alone be the glory. As we gaze through this window, if we can agree with their thoroughly scriptural views, we can breathe a sigh of relief, and walk away with confidence, assurance and a smile on our faces.

Questions for Review.

1. What Scriptures (other than the ones mentioned in this chapter) teach that there is a basic order to salvation?

2. Can you find more Scriptures on the biblical teachings about effectual calling or adoption?

3. From a concordance, do a word study of justification in the

OT. Are there differences in justification in the OT and NT?

4. In that many people are confused about sanctification, from a study of the words *holy*, *saints* and *sanctify*, what biblical insights can you gain?

5. Why is glorification important? What does the Scripture teach about it?

For Discussion.

1. How does the WCF relate the covenant and the work of Christ to the aspects of salvation?

2. Does the teaching of the WCF match your own experience of sanctification?

3. Discuss what happens when we have faulty ideas about perseverance and the assurance of salvation? Are you clear about their basis?

Spotlight: Richard Vines

Richard Vines (1600–1655), following his graduation from Magdalen College, Cambridge, began his service to the Lord as schoolmaster at Hinckley in Leicestershire. His first parish was at Weddington, a village in Warwickshire, where he also faithfully served the small adjacent church at Caldcot until 1642. At the outbreak of the civil war, he also established a public discussion at Nuneaton, seven miles from Coventry, where many traveled to hear his exposition.

An expert in matters of church government, Vines was called "the champion of the [Presbyterian] party in the Assembly, therefore called their Luther." Later he was called to minister to the large parish of Clement's Danes, whose parishioners included the Earl of Essex, a lifelong friend. Vines gave the funeral oration at the Earl's death.

In 1644 Vines was appointed Master of Pembroke-Hall, Cambridge, where he served until 1649. At the Assembly, Vines also served on the Committee of Accommodation and in 1645 was appointed to the committee to prepare the Confession of Faith. One biographer said of him:

> He was mighty in the Scriptures, and an interpreter one of a thousand. He was a great champion in controversy, and eminently distinguished for giving a mortal wound to error. In his powerful and spiritual ministry, he insisted very much upon the all-important doctrine of justification, which he had thoroughly studied; greatly debasing man and exalting the Lord Jesus Christ, and his finished righteousness. Toward the conclusion of his ministry, he discovered much earnestness, in driving man out of himself unto the Savior; throwing down all false foundations of the hope of heaven, and warmly recommending the only sure foundation which Jehovah has laid in Zion. He seriously exhorted his hearers to study heart-holiness and a conversation becoming the gospel of Christ. And he knew well how to speak a word in season to wounded spirits.

As one whose abilities commanded the respect of the king as well as that of his brethren, he was sent by Parliament in 1648 as a member of the delegation negotiating a treaty with the king on the Isle of Wight.

He died in middle age, leaving behind a reputation as an expert in the original language of the New Testament. He was known as "the very prince of preachers, a thorough Calvinist, and a bold honest man, without pride and flattery." One funeral elegy noted the following:

> Our English Luther, Vines, whose death I weep,
> Stole away (and said nothing) in a sleep.
> Sweet (like a swan) he preached the day he went,
> And for his cordial took a sacrament;
> Had it but been suspected he would die,
> His people sure had stopped him with their cry.

His chief written works were *A Treatise…of the Sacrament of the Lord's Supper*, a collection of 20 sermons on the subject (1657), and devotional works such as *Christ A Christian's only Gain* (1661), *God's Drawing, and Man's Coming to Christ* (1662), and *The Saint's Nearness to God* (1662).

7. God's Society

This is the day of new organizations, clubs, and societies almost beyond number, with all sorts of objects and of every name, for men, women, and children. But man has never devised any organization equal to the Church in its educating and uplifting power.[1]

B y their fruits you shall know them." Jesus' words are true not only for individuals, but also for organizations. The church was the chief vehicle that expressed the Westminster Assembly teachings. To gaze through this window, let's find seats inside Westminster Abbey, in the Jerusalem Chamber, and look out the windows as the flow of faith moves into the world through the church.

As the divines adjourn in 1649, let's see where their work leads as an expression of their faith. We will concentrate on the teaching and impact of the Westminster Confession of Faith in three key areas: (1) the church, (2) the sacraments and (3) church government. In each of these areas the Westminster faith had a significant impact.

The Church

In the seventeenth century, long before voluntary societies and para-church groups had been established, the church was the primary organization for expressing and living out the faith.

The "communion of saints," which we profess to believe when we recite the Apostles' Creed, was the foundation for the Westminster Assembly's teaching on the church. Communion of saints occurs when those united by Christ see themselves more as part of the corporate body of Christ than as separate entities. Chapter 26 of the WCF says that "all saints, that are united to Jesus Christ their head, by his Spirit, and by faith, have fellowship with him in his graces, sufferings, death, resurrection, and glory: and, being united to one another in love, they have communion in each other's gifts and graces, and are obliged to the performance of such duties, public and private, as do conduce to their mutual good, both in the inward and outward man" (WCF 26.1). This is consistent with what the Book of Acts represents as the earliest Christian fellowship (Acts 2:45; 4:32). The Assembly understood the church to be God's society.

According to the WCF, saints are encouraged to assist one another in spiritual services so as to build up the body of Christ, even to "relieving each other in outward things, according to their several abilities and necessities" (26.2). This concept provides opportunity for evangelism, and for diaconal ministry, as well as for building up believers. It was the Apostle Paul who encouraged the church to "do good to all people, especially to those who belong to the family of believers" (Gal. 6:10). But the communion of saints does not do away with private ownership of property, as if this were a socialistic society (26.3).

What did the Westminster Assembly think of the church? In WCF, chapter 25, they drew a distinction between the invisible and the visible church, with the invisible church as the sum total of the elect who have been "gathered into one, under Christ the head…and [who] is the spouse, the body, the fulness of him that filleth all in all" (25.1). The most basic definition of the church is that society which is created by God through his strong and sovereign election. The church, therefore, is not defined chiefly in terms of its appearance, structure, sacraments or doctrine, but rather in terms of the work of salvation which God performs for his elect. The whole number of the elect, therefore, is the invisible church.

In contrast, the visible church is the external church (25.2), consisting of all those in the world (that is the meaning of *catholic*) who profess the true religion, as well as their children. The WCF is thoroughly covenantal in including the children of believers in the church. Moreover, this church is the "kingdom of the Lord Jesus Christ, the house and family of God, out of which there is no ordinary possibility of salvation" (25.2). Thus the church is to be that ordinary mechanism which nourishes and accompanies salvation. It was unthinkable to the Assembly that a person might be saved and then not be a part of the household of faith. In addition, to this outward society are given the sacraments, the ministry of preaching, and the duty of building up the saints until Christ returns (25.3).

Individual congregations are more or less pure according to a definite standard: (1) how the Gospel is taught and embraced, (2) how the sacraments are administered, and (3) how public worship is performed (25.4).

It is admitted that even the best churches are "subject both to mixture and error" (25.5). Yet in the midst of this mixture of truth and error, God is faithful, and as the WCF assures, his church will never be left on earth without a witness and without worship to give him glory. Finally the WCF, in stark contrast to the Roman Catholic tradition, explicitly confesses that there is no visible head of the church except the Lord Jesus Christ.

In our age of heightened individualism, the WCF's teaching—that God's sovereignty and salvation results in the saints' inclusion in his society—is a healthy corrective for us. According to the WCF, God puts us in a social entity, a society to grow and serve him. His structured and vital society is the chief vehicle for living out the faith expressed earlier in the WCF. This society then becomes salt and light to the world.

The Sacraments

One of the primary callings and exclusive responsibilities of the church is to administer the sacraments. As the WCF teaches, the sacraments are those directly instituted holy signs and seals of the covenant of grace which Christ has explicitly ordered for the church to carry out until his return (27.1). The uses of the sacraments, according to the WCF authors, were: "to represent Christ and his benefits; and to confirm our interest in him: as also, to put a visible difference between those that belong unto the church, and the rest of the world; and solemnly to engage them to the service of God in Christ, according to his Word" (27.1).

The Westminster divines wanted to make sure that the confusions evident in the Roman Catholic and some Episcopal churches were not perpetuated. They taught that there was a difference between the sign of the sacrament and that for which it stood (27.2). Moreover, they said that any grace that comes through the proper use of the sacraments is a result not of magic power within them, nor of the spiritual piety or ordination of the person who ministers it, but rather is the result of the work of the Holy Spirit and the divine institution of God.

Recognizing the continuity between the Old and New Testaments, the WCF authors confessed that the sacraments of both, as far as spiritual meaning, were basically the same (27.5). In keeping with that, there were only two sacraments (in contrast to the Roman Catholic belief in seven sacraments) viewed by the Assembly as "ordained by Christ our Lord in the gospel" (27.4)—baptism and the Lord's Supper.

In chapter 28, baptism is defined in keeping with the earlier definition of a sacrament as that which was ordained by Christ.

This sign and seal of the covenant of grace signified a person's "ingrafting into Christ, of regeneration, of remission of sins, and of his giving up unto God, through Jesus Christ, to walk in newness of life" (28.1). In keeping with the biblical and apostolic tradition, water was the only element to be used, and baptism was to be ministered in the name of the triune God. The WCF also stated that the total immersion of a person into water was not necessary (28.3), but could be administered by pouring or sprinkling. This was in keeping with the dominant Old Testament mode of sprinkling with a hyssop branch (Ps. 51:7). Not only were adult believers to be baptized, but the infants of one or more believing parents were also to be baptized (WCF 28.4), in keeping with the Old Testament practice of circumcision.

So important was the sacrament of baptism to the WCF authors that they saw it as a "great sin to contemn [hold in contempt] or neglect this ordinance" (28.5); yet, they realized that a person's salvation was not based on this sacrament. They also confessed that baptism represented the Holy Spirit's work in a person's life. In addition, the working power of baptism was not tied to the exact moment in which it was applied (as in an infant's life), but that the grace and promise was delivered in due time by the Holy Spirit to the elect, or as the WCF says, "to such (whether of age or infants) as that grace belongeth unto, according to the counsel of God's own will, in his appointed time" (28.6). Finally the authors of the WCF, in keeping with Ephesians 4, stated that baptism should be applied to a person only once.

In chapter 29 great detail is given on the Lord's Supper, primarily in contrast to the Roman Catholic and hierarchical practices of that time. For example, private masses are ruled out (29.4), as is the denial of the cup to the people, the worshipping of the elements, the adoration of the elements, or the re-sacrifice of Christ in the mass (29.2). In addition, the WCF authors state that transubstantiation (the belief that the elements change their substance from bread and wine into the actual body and blood of Christ) is "repugnant, not to Scripture alone, but even to common sense, and reason" (29.6).

Church Government

Milton remarked that church discipline was "the execution and applying of doctrine home."[2] More discussion, debate and study was devoted to the nature and practice of church government than to any other topic considered by the Assembly. In fact, many commentators on the Westminster Assembly have spoken of the "Grand Debate" as the lengthy and thorough discussion of the principles of church government. Two centuries after the convening of the Assembly, Thomas Smyth of South Carolina summed up the importance of the subject of government by saying that it "became the all-engrossing topic of the day, and, from its close connection with public affairs, a national question."[3] There were diverse views on this subject through the duration of the Assembly. In fact no real compromise on this subject was ever reached. The disunity on this topic apparent during the Assembly continues today.

The two chapters in the WCF on church government (30 and 31) are slim for two reasons: first, the committees formulating the WCF (and the Assembly itself) could not agree on a wide range of propositions on church government, although the primary skeletal structure of biblical Presbyterianism is clearly the view of the vast majority; and, second, the WCF here as elsewhere exhibits the commitment of the divines not to exceed the bounds of scriptural revelation on a particular topic.

In chapter 30, it is affirmed first that Christ as king and head of his church has erected a government for his society—a specific church government distinct from the civil government (30.1). Within this church government, Christ has ordained certain leaders and has given to them the keys of the kingdom (Matt. 16:19; 18:18). To these church elders are given the power, which Christ spoke of, to declare that sins are forgiven or not (John 20:23). Moreover, to these leaders is the ministry of the gospel and church discipline given.

Fifty years before the Westminster Assembly, Thomas Cartwright, an early British Presbyterian, expressed the basis for this orderly discipline this way: "The discipline of Christ's church that is necessary for all times is delivered by Christ, and set down in the holy Scriptures. Therefore the true and lawful discipline is to be fetched from thence, and from thence alone. And that which resteth upon any other foundation ought to be esteemed unlawful and counterfeit. Of all particular churches there is one and the same right order and form: therefore also no one may challenge to itself any power over others; nor any right which doth not alike agree to others."[4]

Church discipline is often ignored in modern churches, but it was not so in the seventeenth century. The WCF authors recognized and taught the necessity of church discipline "for the reclaiming and gaining of offending brethren, for deterring of others from the like offenses, for purging out of that leaven which might infect the whole lump, for vindicating the honor of Christ, and the holy profession of the gospel, and for preventing the wrath of God which might justly fall upon the church" should it continue in disobedience (30.3).

A study of Scripture will reveal church discipline to be an undeniable duty both to individuals and to the church. (See Matt. 18:15–18; Titus 3:10; 1 Cor. 5; 1 Tim. 5:20; 1:20.) The purposes of church discipline are never to glorify the elders or to seek vengeance, but to reclaim a Christian brother (Gal. 6:1).

The WCF sets out the modes of church discipline as admonition, suspension from the Lord's Supper and excommunication, according to the nature of the crime and the behavior of the person (30.4). The topic of church discipline was hotly debated at the Westminster Assembly, because it was realized that if authority truly had been given by Christ to these officers (as Presbyterianism had long asserted) then there was a type of authority given to the church that was not given to individuals. The few Independents at the Assembly sought to relegate the church's authority to an advisory role, but the majority of the Assembly refuted that, holding fast to their view that believers should be submissive to their officers (1 Pet. 5:1–5), and, moreover, that Christ had indeed given more than a mere counseling or advisory power to the church.

The Westminster divines knew that if the church were to grow in a depraved world, it must carry out church discipline in obedience to her Master. If we neglect church discipline today, it is because we fear society's rejection or worry that our church growth might be inhibited (cf. Acts 4, 5), or perhaps because we are lazy. Church discipline was non-negotiable to the church 350 years ago, and as we commemorate this Assembly we should revive this essential mark of the church today. Discipline and structure are essential for any society to continue or maintain virtue. God's society has been given its own order.

Another part of church government was the relationship of different levels of governing bodies. According to the WCF, to expedite government and to build up the church, God had ordained assemblies, called synods or councils (31.1). These were not to be confused with the civil government.

According to the WCF, these ecclesiastical councils were not to meddle in state affairs, except to give their humble and biblical advice (31.5). Rather they were to decide controversial matters of faith or conscience. When an assembly decided cases or made decrees, as long as they were in keeping with the Word of God, they were to be received with reverence and submission, because they agreed with the Word of God and because of the cumulative effect of the many advisors giving council (31.3). This is God's society at work.

Assembly participant Robert Baillie made these comments on the importance of church order:

> Now indeed, every monster walks in the street without control, while all ecclesiastic government is cast asleep; this too long inter-reign and mere anarchy hath invited every unclean creature to creep out of its cave, and shew in public its mishapen face to all who like to behold. But, if once the government of Christ were set up amongst us, as it is in the rest of the reformed churches, we know not what would impede it...to banish out of the land these spirits of error, in all meekness, humility, and love...truth convincing and satisfying the minds of the seduced. Episcopal courts were never fitted for the reclaiming of minds....But the reformed Presbytery doth proceed in a spiritual method evidently fitted for the gaining of hearts....Let England once be countenanced by her [i.e., presbyterian courts] superior powers, to enjoy the just and necessary liberty of consistories for congregation, of presbyteries for counties....Put these holy and divine instruments in the hand of the Church of England, by the blessing of God thereupon, the sore and great evil of so many heresies and schisms shall quickly be cured."[5]

The essential principles of Presbyterianism were debated at length by the Westminster Assembly. Following the normal committee format for reporting, what follows is a summary of the major propositions recommended by the second and third committees: "In inquiring after the officers belonging to the Church of the New Testament, we first find that Christ, who is Priest, Prophet, King, and Head of the Church, hath fullness of power, and containeth all other offices, by way of eminency, in himself; and therefore hath many of their names attributed to him." The following names of Church officers were mentioned as given in Scripture to Christ: apostle; pastor; bishop; teacher;

minister, or *diakonos*; but this last name was rejected by the Assembly, as not meaning a Church officer in the Scripture passage where it is used. The report of the third committee was similar, ascribing, in Scripture terms, the government to Jesus Christ, who, being ascended far above all heavens, "hath given all officers necessary for the edification of his Church; some whereof are extraordinary, some ordinary."[6] In Scripture they found the following officers: apostles, evangelists, prophets, pastors, teachers, bishops or overseers, presbyters or elders, deacons and widows.

These principles became the primary carriers of the underlying beliefs of the church. They were the outward manifestation, the organized vehicle of communicating the faith. The Westminster Directory of Government summarizes its scriptural basis, in terms of Christ:

Jesus Christ, upon whose shoulder the government is, whose name is called Wonderful, Counsellor, the Mighty God, the Everlasting Father, the Prince of Peace; of the increase of whose government and peace there shall be no end; who sits upon the throne of David, and upon his kingdom, to order it, and establish it with judgment and justice, from henceforth even for ever; having all power given unto him in heaven and earth by the Father, who raised him from the dead, and set him at his own right hand, far above all principality and power, and might, and dominion, and every name that is named, not only in this world, but also in that which is to come: and put all things under his feet, and gave him to be head over all things to the church, which is his body, the fullness of him that filleth all in all: he being ascended up far above all heavens, that he might fill all things, received gifts for his church, and gave all officers necessary for the edification of his church, and perfecting of his saints.

116

The London divines met as a presbytery every Monday to consider means for enlarging the kingdom. Based on the Company of Pastors in Geneva (the presbytery in Calvin's time), with a weekly meeting, the province of London was subdivided into 12 presbyteries. Each consisted of from 12–15 churches, and as to governmental structure, was nearly identical to the presbyteries we have today. The main exception was in the ratio of ministers to ruling elders; each of the London presbyteries were composed of 12 ministers and 24 ruling elders. After the Westminster Assembly, and until 1659, these functioning presbyteries met twice a week and sought ways to reform the church and spread the kingdom.

A study of Acts 15 yields biblical support for the Presbyterian form of government as incorporated in the Westminster Standards. God's society is no slipshod organization. He made it, and it is his church. Thus it should be implemented his way. God loved this church very much. Not only did he give his Son for her, but further, he gave her a continuing government and method of problem solving, which is exhibited in Scripture.

The first pastoral letter in church history (Acts 15:23–29) is from "the apostles and elders...to the Gentile believers in Antioch, Syria, and Cilicia." Those locales tell us that the drafters of this document did not envision themselves making decisions for only one locale, on a case-by-case basis. The church, headed by Jesus Christ, was not designed to be a society with different doctrines tailored to the fickle tastes of individuals. She was one body and this decision was for the entire church, in all locations. The underlying view is that Christians everywhere would want to heed the wisdom of this decree. Absent from this record is the assumption that each church would do as it pleased on questions. These were standards by the whole church, for the whole society. It was a unified spiritual society with the same beliefs and practices, not just a consortium of loosely affiliated churches. The decision of the Assembly of Jerusalem was for all churches.

Many modern Christians strive fervently for independence. This was not the desire of the New Testament church (1 Cor. 7:17; 11:16; 14:33–38). Were they wrong? Or are we? Is it possible that we yearn for too much independence and self-rule? Recall that Adam and Eve started the movement to be independent. Scripture corrects and rebukes the desire of a church to do what it wishes.

The church of 1 Corinthians was one holy, universal church. It was not a series of diverse franchises, each of which pursued its own ends, programs and impulses. Hence, this pastoral letter was intended for all Christians. Only if the church has an underlying oneness does a letter like 1 Corinthians make sense. This letter was received not merely as advice, but rather as the settled, deliberated standard of the church—and the Christians submitted to its wisdom. It was for the whole church, not just some parts.

In 1641, Alexander Henderson had summarized Presbyterianism by saying: "In the authority of these assemblies, parochial, presbyterial, provincial, and national, and in the subordination of the lesser unto the greater, or of the more particular elderships to the larger and general eldership, doth consist the order, strength, and steadfastness of the Church of Scotland....Here is a superiority without tyranny, for no minister hath a papal or monarchical jurisdiction over his own flock, far less over other pastors and over the congregations of a large diocese. Here there is parity without confusion and disorder....Every particular church is subordinate to the presbytery, the presbytery to the synod, and the synod to the national assembly...here there is a subjection without slavery."[7]

The motive behind the Westminster Assembly's views on government was to preserve the integrity of the gospel, to build up the flock of Christ, and to propagate the good news of Jesus. The Assembly saw the governmental provisions of the WCF as means to that end, and their sole motive in laying these out was to exalt Christ and further the work of God's society. The main mark on cultures has come through this organized society and its individuals.

The seventeenth century poet John Donne said: "The place then where we take our degrees in this knowledge of God, our Academy, our University for that, is the Church...the ordinary place for Degrees is the University, and the ordinary place for Illumination in the knowledge of God, is the Church...the Church is our Academy, there we must be bred."

Let us recommit ourselves to God's society; as the hymn "I Love Thy Kingdom, Lord" expresses:

I love thy church, O God: her walls before thee stand,
Dear as the apple of thine eye, and graven on thy hand.
For her my tears shall fall, for her my prayers ascend;
To her my cares and toils be giv'n, till toils and cares shall
    end.

Questions for Review.

1. Can you find Scriptures that define the church based on God's action, rather than man's?

2. What is the "communion of saints" according to Scripture and the WCF?

3. What is the biblical basis for (a) baptism and (b) the Lord's Supper? Does your church's practice conform to the teaching of Westminster in these areas?

4. From a study of Scriptures on church discipline, why do we need such discipline?

5. Besides Acts 15, can you find other scriptural passages that support the Presbyterian form of government?

For Discussion.

1. Why was the church so important in the seventeenth century? Should it be today?

2. Why is the distinction between the visible and invisible church important?

3. Do you think the divines overemphasized government and discipline? Why? How is government the "execution and applying of doctrine home" (Milton)?

Spotlight: John Dury

John Dury (1596–1680) was born in Scotland and began his studies at Sedan (in France), entering Oxford in 1624. He was fluent in French and German and became conversant in several other language groups used within the Reformed family. His lifelong passion was to promote reconciliation, first between Calvinists and Lutherans, and then among other groups throughout the Christian world.

In 1634 he published a plan of union which he circulated among various Christian groups in Scotland, England, Germany, Transylvania, Sweden and Denmark. Many of the continental Reformed divines expressed favor regarding this plan. He also communicated this plan to leaders in New England who heartily approved. Richard Baxter observed: "Mr. Dury, having spent thirty years in his endeavors to reconcile the Lutherans and Calvinists, was again going abroad upon that work, and desired the judgment of our association how it might be most successfully accomplished."

With all the controversies and eventual divisions in the Reformed family, it is helpful to see that there were peacemakers like Dury in the Assembly. Dury was a man of amiable character who was greatly respected even by his opponents. He indefatigably labored in the pursuit of Christian unity, taking to heart the scriptural admonition in Ephesians 4, which stresses that it is a diligent labor, requiring much work, to keep the unity of the gospel in the bond of peace. One of Dury's letters to the Lord Chancellor Hide in July 1660 summarizes his life's goal:

> My Lord, In the application which I made to your honor when you were at the Hague, I offered the fruit of my thirty years labors towards healing the breaches of Protestants; and this I did as one who never had served the turn of any party, or have been biased by particular interests for any advantage to myself; but walking in the light by rules and principles, have stood free from all in matters of strife, to be able to serve through love. My way hath been, and is, to solicit the means of peace and truth among the dissenting parties, to do good offices, and to quiet their discontents, and I must still continue in this way if I should be useful. But not being rightly understood in my aims and principles, I have been constrained to give this brief account thereof, as well to rectify the misconstructions of former actings, as to prevent farther mistakes concerning my way...and wherein I hope to persevere unto the end, as the Lord shall enable me, to be without offence unto all, with a sincere purpose to approve myself to his Majesty in all faithfulness.

Dury left behind numerous writings and his pursuit of unity did not discourage strength of principle. Dury wrote *A Model of Church Government* (1647), and *Seasonable Discourse...for*

Reformation (1649). He also wrote *A Peace-maker Without partiality and Hypocrisy, or the Gospel Way* (1648), and *The Unchanged, Constant, and Single-hearted Peace-maker drawn forth into the world: or, A Vindication of John Dury from the aspersions cast upon him in a nameless Pamphlet* (1650). Dury provides an example of a peacemaker in pursuit of a comprehensive union.

8. Influence of the Assembly

> Whether evaluated by the work it did, or by the influence which these Presbyterian standards have had throughout the world...the Westminster Assembly was the most important Protestant Assembly that ever met.[1]

To see the influence of the Westminster Assembly, we must enter the Abbey, and look outward across years and nations. The standard measurement of influence is Jesus' own: "By their fruit you will recognize them" (Matt. 7:20).

Let's take a look at the Assembly's influence in general, and then how it has affected the church, the family and civil government.

We should also agree that these divines' influence should not be exaggerated. As Mitchell comments: "We do not claim for them perfection or infallibility. They were men; and were subject to human infirmities, and were infected with some of the prejudices of the age in which they lived, which is more or less true of all men."[2]

A High Tide of Influence

William Hetherington called Westminster "the most important event in the century in which it occurred; and...it has exerted, and...will yet exert, a far more wide and permanent influence upon both the civil and the religious history of mankind than has generally been even imagined." In some respects the Assembly was a product of its age; nevertheless, it is properly recognized as a landmark in British church history "like the culminating point in a range of lofty and scarred hills, themselves the outcome of deep seated combustion."[3]

Toward the end of the nineteenth century, a defender for the lasting influence of the Westminster standards said that

> for purity of doctrine...for condensation of great truths expressed in the fewest words, these Standards, by the admission of those who have no sympathy with Presbyterianism, are unrivalled among all uninspired writings. They gather up the cardinal truths enunciated through all the ages and present them in the most concise form. Their superiority consists not in the originality of the truths themselves, but in condensing what was best in all the theological systems of the past, and presenting them in the truest and most intelligible form. We may say of the Westminster Standards what was said of the proverbial philosophy of many generations: "The truth, though old and oft expressed, is his at last who says it best."[4]

In the late 1800's, Warfield contended that as an accurate and vital compilation of Christian truth, the WCF was

> the product of intellect working only under the impulse of the heart, and must be a monument of the religious life. This is true of all the great creedal statements, and pre-eminently true of the Westminster Standards. Their authors were men of learning and philosophic grasp; but above all of piety. Their interest was not in speculative construction, but in the protection of their flocks from deadly error....In pro-

portion as our own religious life flows in a deep and broad stream, in that proportion will we find spiritual delight in the Westminster Standards.[5]

When Warfield saw attempts to lessen the influence of the WCF and lower its standard, he felt "an inexpressible grief [to see the Church] spending its energies in a vain attempt to lower its testimony to suit the ever-changing sentiment of the world about it."[6]

Citing another great nineteenth century Calvinist, and calling the church to arms, Warfield wrote (1892) of the need to preserve this influence: "Mr. Spurgeon put it in even sharper figure, we shall never satisfy the pursuing wolves that seek to destroy our whole system by flinging them our children to devour. The Church would be more at her proper business in whetting her weapons rather than in dulling them. It is not a time in which to whisper the truth in doubtful phrases, but to shout it from the housetops in the clearest and sharpest language in which it can be framed."[7]

British writer Iain Murray, notes the influence of the WCF, and the need in our own times to have an objective measure of orthodoxy:

The Westminster Confession is being sold and read, in various editions, around the world to an extent which would have been regarded by many as unthinkable fifty years ago. Yet this ought not to be surprising because, ultimately, there can be only two alternatives in an evangelical understanding of the Christian Faith, the Calvinistic and the Arminian. The Church has passed through an era in which the Arminian understanding has held sway and its effects in evangelism, in worship and in Christian living have had opportunity to be worked out fully. We are again, in history, at a turning point.[8]

Influence on Preaching

Moreover, as to the enduring value of the work of Westminster as a companion for preaching, Robert Coyle cheered:

> I cannot but long for a revival to some extent of doctrinal preaching that shall follow the general type of theological thinking set before us in our standards...close adherence to the essential thoughts of our Confession can scarcely fail to give...hearers a grander, nobler, truer, and more scriptural conception of God, than many of them are now forming under a style of preaching that is better adapted to give a conception of the character of modern leaders and events.[9]

At the 250th anniversary of the Assembly one commentator said,

> The forces that make history are usually not conspicuous. The mightiest things are not those which appeal to the eye of sense. In this great world-drama there are actors behind the scenes far more potent than those that stand close up against the foot-lights. However insignificant they may have seemed...and however small may be the space allotted to them by the mere secular historian, we now know that the battles fought in the Jerusalem Chamber were more significant than Naseby or Marston Moor....It was these principles...that made the Westminster Assembly the most important event of the seventeenth century.[10]

Nor are these merely past sentiments, true only for an earlier age: "These principles are not dead. Principles that involve the glory of the Son of God, the independence of the Church, the infallibility of his Word, the freedom of conscience, the spirituality of worship, can never die. They are the most living issues of this present hour. Today they need ringing out more faithfully than ever."[11] G. K. Chesterton issued a biting reminder as to the timelessness of real truth:

> An imbecile habit has arisen in modern controversy of saying that such and such a creed can be held in one age but cannot be held in another. Some dogma, we are told, was credible in the twelfth century, but is not credible in the twentieth. You might as well say that a certain philosophy can be believed on Mondays, but cannot be believed on Tuesdays. You might as well say of a view of the cosmos that it was suitable to half-past three, but not suitable to half-past four. What a man can believe depends upon his philosophy, not upon the clock or the century. If a man believes in unalterable natural law, he cannot believe in any miracle in any age. If a man believes in a will behind law, he can believe in any miracle in any age.[12]

On the benefit of reviving the influence of these truths, Robert Coyle urged:

> What we need to multiply conversions, to make our preaching mighty, to kindle our missionary fires, to set every Board free from the incubus of debt, to bring us together, North and South, to unite the entire Presbyterian family, and send us forth upon a new career of conquest and glory, is a revival of loyalty to our King. What is needed is to get away from side issues, away from the catching themes of the hour, away from themes literary, and themes political, and themes social, and themes exploited by the daily press, and lift up the name of our King, and make it pre-eminent above every name. Unless this is done, agnosticism and materialism will win the day. Unless this is done, the pulpit will go into eclipse.[13]

Unity

Often overlooked is the fact that the Westminster standards can foster unity:

Some do not like creeds; but our Church has always thought it fair and honorable to state explicitly what it understands the Word of God to teach. Our Creed then is our witness-bearer to the whole world. Indeed, no man can write or preach a sermon without stating in part his creed, and we are bound to contend earnestly for the faith once delivered to the saints. At the same time our Creed is pre-eminently an irenical document, and we believe the clear, definite statement by the Christian denominations of what they believe, is the very best road to an ultimate agreement of the churches on the fundamental and essential doctrines of our holy religion.[14]

The hope for a unity around biblical summaries in the WCF was expressed:

With a creed and polity adapted to the conversion of the world to Christ, and to the consolidation of the churches of the world in one grand representative organism, our Church is bent on the gathering of all the friends of Christ into a glorious Solidarity—the Kingdom of God—embracing all the true followers of the King of kings; for it believes that this consummated fact and this unparalleled glory of the Church of Christ are foreordained of God, and that his plan shall not be frustrated by the powers of darkness.[15]

Influence on the Family and Child-rearing

The influence of the documents such as the Shorter Catechism, the people's creed, cast a long shadow. As Thomas Carlyle said: "The older I grow—and I now stand upon the brink of eternity—the more comes back to me the first sentence in the Catechism which I learned when a child, and the fuller and deeper its meaning becomes: What is the chief end of man? To glorify God, and to enjoy Him forever."[16]

One fruit of Westminster is its influence on discipling the family. The Westminster tradition placed a premium on godly parents instructing their covenant children in the principles of the true religion through the catechism. Disciples of this Assembly have always taken Proverbs 22:6 to heart, and have sought to train their children in the way they should go. These made the most of the proverb: As the twig is bent, the tree is inclined.

On the value of the Catechisms and early memorization, the following was held out 100 years ago as the potential for the influence of the Catechism on our youth:

"1. Unless they are learned in childhood and youth, the strong probability is that they will never be learned at all. Not one in five hundred of our people, perhaps, learns them later in life. They must be learned, then, early in life, or never. Are we willing for the latter alternative? Are we willing that our children shall never *accurately* know the great truths of religion? Are we willing that they shall never accurately know what is meant by such doctrines as faith, and repentance, and justification, and sanctification? Would that be wise? Would that be safe?

"2. We cannot too early impress the great truths of the Catechisms on their minds and hearts. We should never forget that in childhood and youth the soul is most susceptible of deep and lasting impressions...most susceptible of impressions for good or evil; and then, as the years elapse, those souls, with those impressions on them, indurate; and thus those impressions become as lasting, as everlasting, it may be, as the souls themselves. How important it is, then, that these earliest and most enduring impressions should be made in behalf of right and truth and God by the inculcation of the great truths of our Catechisms! How important that those truths should, in the very beginning of their histories, be laid down deep around the very roots of their young natures, that up out of them their future characters may grow, and that by them their future lives may be determined and controlled!

"3. It is necessary to our success as a denomination that our Catechisms be intelligently and faithfully taught. Our doctrines are constantly and bitterly assailed. In much of the literature of the day, especially in that kind which, unfortunately, our children too much read, they are caricatured as severe, harsh, unreasonable, antiquated; as belonging to a remote and ignorant past; as being entirely out of harmony with the progress that has been made in better views of the benevolence, of the divine nature, of the dignity of man, and of the vastness and freeness of redeeming love. Multitudes of our people do not know how to meet these assaults....Why cannot the ministers and officers in our denomination so instruct our people as to these great doctrines, that in every church there shall be a number, at least, who shall know how to maintain them against any of the popular assaults that are so frequently made upon them? We shall never succeed as we may and ought until this is done."[17]

The Directory for Family Worship, written in 1647, shows us most clearly the strong views of the family held by the Scottish commissioners present at the Assembly. This document laid out directions for building up faith, cherishing piety, maintaining unity, and deterring schism in godly families. So important was this family faith that the Scottish General Assembly even called upon Presbyteries to require those within their bounds to carry these things out under threat of discipline, and, moreover, that every individual family was to practice family worship. If a family neglected family worship, "the head of the family is to be first admonished privately to amend his fault;

and, in case of his continuing therein, he is to be gravely and sadly reproved by the session; after which reproof, if he be found still to neglect Family-worship, let him be, for his obstinacy in such an offence, suspended and debarred from the Lord's supper, as being justly esteemed unworthy to communicate therein, till he amend."

Influence on Civil Government

The Reformation truths contained in the WCF have had a wide influence in the theory and practice of government. Cultures spawned from the Reformation saw the imprint of Reformed thought on the underlying ideas about the state. In 1943, at the 300th anniversary of the Assembly, J. McDowell Richards said, "It is the glory of the Presbyterian system as set forth by the Westminster divines that it has produced citizens of intelligence, of integrity, of courage."[18]

The Westminster authors gave to western civilization a comprehensive view of Christian liberty as well as a properly defined role relationship between the church and state. The WCF's chapter on civil government teaches that in his authority as supreme Lord and King, God has also ordained a distinct civil government for the world. Yet the WCF is quick to disallow any sphere of human activity outside of the sovereignty of God, noting that even the ordained civil government is to be "under him, over the people, for his own glory, and the public good" (WCF 23.1). Thus has God given the civil magistrate all of the biblical tools for carrying out the Christian government. In addition, it is acceptable or lawful for Christians to serve in government offices (23.2), despite the contention by some Christians that to do so was a violation of Christian conscience.

The duty of Christians toward the magistrate, as laid out in Scripture, is to pray for them, to honor them, to pay taxes (Rom. 13), to obey lawful commands, and to give unto their religious leaders all service and assistance they can, however recognizing that even the most powerful of human leaders may violate some part of God's command. This is one of the legacies of Westminster.

In the WCF, chapter 23, governments are prohibited from taking to themselves the matters of church, including the administration of the Word and sacraments and exercising church discipline. Instead they are to serve as "nursing fathers" to protect members of the church without giving preference to any particular denomination. (This is the true meaning of the first amendment to the U.S. Constitution in not giving preference to any "establishment of religion.") The role of the civil government is to allow freedom for the church functionaries to carry out their roles without danger and violence, and the state is not to interfere with or hinder the proper exercise of faith by Christians. It is also the duty of the civil magistrates to protect all people and to allow their freedom of religious expression (23.3).

This view of the role of the church and state became a foundation for western civilization. As to its influence in protecting and preserving common civil liberties, one historian noted, "Should ever the time come when the liberties of the people are assailed, either on the one side by civil and ecclesiastical despotism, or on the other by anarchy and license, they will find no clearer declaration of their sacred rights, and no better rock on which to plant their feet in their defense, than the Westminster Confession of Faith."[19]

It is perhaps only after the centuries that we see the great donation of the Westminster Assembly in this doctrine of civil liberties. Hetherington observed:

> Presbytery awoke, and has begun her hallowed work of instructing her own people. While she offers her cordial fellowship to all who love her Divine and only Head, the inference is obvious, and may be thus

stated: When the vital spirit of Prelacy is inert, it becomes comparatively harmless: when the vital spirit of Presbytery is inert, or repressed, it becomes oppressive. Again, when the vital spirit of Prelacy is active, it becomes despotic and persecuting, intolerant and illiberal: when the vital spirit of Presbytery is active, it becomes gracious and compassionate, tolerant of everything but sin, and generous to all who believe the truth and love the Savior. Let the thoughtful reader say, which system is of human, and which of divine institution,—which shows a spirit of the earth, earthly, and which, of heavenly origin and character.[20]

A few summations may give us a renewed appreciation. As to timelessness, Mitchell says,

Half-learned theologians are very apt to boast of having struck out new light, when the same opinions had been vented, discussed, and refuted, long before they were born. As far as we have observed, every attempt to improve on the system here so clearly laid down, and deduced from Scripture, has been an utter failure. Not that the Westminster divines discovered these doctrines: they never pretended to have found out anything new. They aimed to teach simply and plainly, what had been received from the beginning. Their greatest abhorrence was of innovations in religion....Although this system of doctrine is repulsive to the pride of man, and which carnal reason does not readily receive...yet whenever true religion is received, and men are led seriously to study the word of God, they almost invariably adopt this system, for two reasons: first, because they cannot but see, that these doctrines are plainly taught in the Scriptures; and secondly, because their own experience leads them to the same conclusions.[21]

In closing, John Murray said:

Language fails to assess the blessing that God in His sovereign providence and grace bestowed upon His church through these statements of the Christian faith. The influence exerted by them is beyond all human calculation. We should indeed be remiss if we did not make this [commemoration] the occasion for grateful remembrance of God's inestimable favor. Other men labored and we have entered into their labors. Truly the lines are fallen unto us in pleasant places and we have a goodly heritage.[22]

Questions for Review.

1. How accurately does "by their fruits you shall know them" serve as a standard of evaluation?

2. Does Jude 3 indicate that God's truth will change over time?

3. Can you recall a few instances where the fingerprint of Westminster left its influence?

4. In your own life, how can these standards help in family life or child-rearing?

5. Why did the principles of Westminster have such a broad influence in civil and political arenas?

For Discussion.

1. How can a common confession serve to expedite unity among Christians?

2. How could a better understanding of the work of Westminster help in (a) preaching, (b) officer training, or (c) among the congregation?

3. Why is it so important to begin Scripture and catechism memory when children are young? Have you seen good examples of this?

Spotlight: Herbert Palmer

Herbert Palmer (1601–1647) was born into a family of wealth and nobility. He was nurtured in the faith by his parents and came to have a great love for Scriptures in early childhood. He also learned French which would later be useful for him in his ministry. When he announced that he would become a minister, some of his friends tried to discourage him by telling him that ministers of Christ were hated and despised. Young Palmer responded that that was no concern for him, for the love of God was more of his concern than the opinion of man. This was one minister who counted the costs before entering the ministry.

Accepted at Cambridge in 1615, he graduated Master of Arts in 1622, and the following year became a fellow of Queen's College there. He was ordained to the gospel ministry in 1624. Beginning in 1626 he served in the ministry at the Alphage Church in Canterbury. On several occasions his small stature and youthful look led his audience to be surprised by the depths of his preaching and teaching ministry. Many benefited from his ministry, and his speech, like that of a disciple of Christ, was seasoned with grace, sweetness and courtesy. He also corresponded with, and encouraged, many Christians. On occasion he preached to the French congregation in Canterbury, drawing upon his earlier acquired fluency in French.

In 1632 he accepted a call to a church in Ashwell in

Hartfordshire. His desire, while in the ministry, was to free his people from ignorance, and by his constant and zealous exposition, to have them intimately acquainted with their Bibles. While at Ashwell he published a catechism entitled, *An endeavor of making the Principles of the Christian Religion...plain and easy* (1640, and a number of times reprinted) which was one of the prototypes of the Westminster Shorter Catechism; thus dubbing Palmer the "Father of the Shorter Catechism."

Palmer's motto could have been, "true religion will be family religion." Palmer's family was exemplary and his house was characterized by an eminent sense of religion, so much so that it was seen as a school of religion. He was regularly in family worship twice a day, not excusing family members from worship. He also catechized his own family twice a week. After every meal his servants had some portion of Scripture and part of some major religious treatise read to them.

In 1632, having completed his Bachelor of Divinity, he became one of the preachers to students at Cambridge. In 1643 he became a pastor of New Church, Westminster. In 1644 Palmer was elected as a master of Queen's College under the sponsorship of the Earl of Manchester. In this role of administrative leadership for the college, he was very careful to maintain that no person should be admitted to scholarship or fellowship, who was not religious as well as learned.

Palmer wrote several books, the best known of which is a two-volume work on the Christian Sabbath (written jointly with Daniel Cawdrey), published separately in 1642 and 1652. Palmer inherited a large estate, yet he chose a humble life to serve his Master, maintaining and sponsoring several poor scholars of his own while they were studying. While faithfully participating in the Westminster Assembly, he frequently preached to Parliament, stating that honor in this way: "that he did not in that place preach before them, *as before a judge,* but to them authoritatively, as by commission from God. And how much soever they might be superior to him in other respects, yet he was in that place superior to them, as acting in God's name; and therefore would not be afraid to speak, whatever was the will of God and he should tell them, notwithstanding any displeasure or danger which might by this means befall him for so doing." Palmer knew our Lord's words: "When you are brought before...rulers and authorities...the Holy Spirit will teach you what you should say" (Luke 12:12).

9. The Spirituality of the Assembly

"There never was a system since the world stood which put upon man such motives to holiness, or which builds batteries which sweep the whole ground of sin with such terrible artillery." As a matter of fact, wherever this system of truth has been embraced it has produced a noble and distinct type of character— a type so clearly marked that secular historians, with no religious bias, have recognized it, and pointed to it as a "remarkable illustration of the power of religious training in the formation of character."[1]

The Westminster divines have been characterized, by those who have not understood or agreed with them, as devoid of feeling, compassion or spirituality. A simple historical review will show that this simply is not true. On the contrary, they were deeply spiritual and might serve as examples for us today.

The biographer James Reid says of the group: "There were never...men...holier then the...Puritans and Nonconformists of this period. Their piety and devotedness to God were very remarkable....They spent their lives in sufferings, in fastings, in prayers, in walking closely with God in their families, and among their people....They were indefatigably zealous in their Master's service."[2]

However, to balance Reid's words, reflect again on Mitchell's comments: "We do not claim for them perfection or infallibility. They were men; and were subject to human infirmities...."[3]

From the outset of the Assembly, the participants wanted it known how unworthy they were, and, correspondingly, how much they depended on the grace of God from first to last. In the wording of the Solemn League and Covenant, adopted first in Scotland, and later introduced on August 17, 1643 to the Assembly:

> We profess...our unfeigned desire to be humbled for our own sins...especially that we have not as we ought valued the inestimable benefit of the gospel; that we have not labored for the purity and power thereof; and that we have not endeavored to receive Christ in our hearts, nor to walk worthy of him in our lives; which are the cause of other sins and transgressions so much abounding amongst us; and our true and unfeigned purpose, desire, and endeavor for ourselves, and all others under our charge...to amend our lives, and each one to go before another in the example of a real reformation; that the Lord may turn away his wrath and heavy indignation, and establish these churches and kingdoms in truth and peace.[4]

In an early sermon before the Assembly (July 7, 1643), Matthew Newcomen, one of the London supporters of the divine mandate for Presbyterianism, said, "Verily I have often from my heart wished that your greatest adversaries and traducers [critics] might be witnesses of your learned, grave, and pious debates."[5] Newcomen pled with the divines to behave, so that if an unbeliever were to enter during their debates, he might "worship God and report that God is in you of a truth,"[6] an obvious reference to what Paul taught in 1 Corinthians 14:24.

The genuine piety of the membership of the Assembly is exemplified in Philip Nye's speech urging adoption of the Solemn League and Covenant. Speaking of the fear of the Lord, the humility requisite for their task, and the necessary simplicity of spirit, Nye exhorted, "I beseech you, let it be seriously considered, if you mean to do any such work in the house of God as this is; if you mean to pluck up what many years ago was planted, or to build up what so long ago was pulled down, and to go through with this work, and not be discouraged, you must beg of the Lord this excellent spirit, this resolute stirring spirit, otherwise you will be outspirited, and both you and your cause slighted and dishonored."[7]

The work would be tough, and would require spiritual fortitude. Yet, in that delicate balance of spiritual maturity, Nye went on to charge, "We must labor for humility, prudence, gentleness, meekness. A man may be very much zealous and resolute, and yet very meek and merciful: Jesus Christ was a Lion and yet a Lamb also."[8] These were hearts held out sincerely and promptly to serve God. These were not sterile academics; rather they had a passionate zeal for the Lord's honor.

The spirituality of the divines could also be seen in their humble dependence on God and in the prominence they gave to prayer. Daily sessions were opened and closed with prayer, and often interspersed with prayer for specifics. Once a month business was suspended, so that a day of fasting and prayer might be observed in concert with Parliament.

On May 17, 1644 the Assembly adjourned to fast and pray for the needs of the nation and the army. According to Baillie, the "sweetest day ever seen in England" saw the divines begin a day of prayer with Dr. Twisse leading, followed by two hours of prayers by Mr. Marshall, confessing the sins of the Assembly in a passionate, yet prudent manner. The fast continued with preaching by John Arrowsmith, succeeded by another two-hour prayer by Mr. Vines. Another sermon was offered, and yet another two-hour prayer was offered by Mr. Seaman. This particular fast led Baillie to say, "God was so evidently in all this exercise, that we expect certainly a blessing both in our matter...and in the whole kingdom."[9]

"We had hoped that our winter had been past"

Early on, the Assembly corresponded with Reformed churches in Belgium, France and Switzerland. In one letter, the divines disclosed their hearts' passion in terms of spiritual warfare:

> We doubt not, but the sad reports of the miseries under which the church and kingdom of England do bleed...is long since come to your ears; and it is probable, the same instruments of Satan and Antichrist have, by their emissaries, endeavored to present us as black as may be among yourselves....We hoped through the goodness of God...that our winter had been past, yet alas! we find it to be quite otherwise. We know our sins have deserved all, and if we die and perish, the Lord is righteous; to his hand we submit, and to him alone we look for healing. The same antichristian faction not being discouraged, by their want of success in Scotland, have stirred up a bloody rebellion in Ireland, wherein above one hundred thousand Protestants have been destroyed in one province....[We crave] your fervent prayers, both public and private, that God would bring salvation to us; that the blessings of truth and peace may rest upon us; that these three nations may be joined as one stick in the hands of the Lord, and that we ourselves, contemptible builders, called to repair the house of God...may see the pattern of this house, and may...establish uniformity among ourselves; that all mountains may become plains before them and us; that then all who now see the plummet in our hands, may also behold the top-stone set upon the head of the Lord's house among us, and may help us with shouting to cry Grace, grace, to it.[10]

This letter exhibits the fervor, prayerfulness, desire for deep unity, servanthood, and desire to further the glory of God of the Assembly. Remember that the WCF was written by flesh-and-blood Christians familiar with spiritual battles (see Eph. 6:10–13).

The Directory for Worship produced by this Assembly included separate chapters on fasting and thanksgiving, so important were they as spiritual basics. The original drafts of these were drawn up by Goodwin (fasting) and the moderator, Herle (thanksgiving).

As the sufferings of the assemblymen intensified, so did the passion of their preaching. One unsympathetic poet described Assembly member Edmund Calamy's imprisonment for the faith at Newgate as it was exhibited in his preaching style:

Dead, and yet preach! these Presbyterian slaves
Will not give over preaching in their graves....
this felony deserved imprisonment;
Why can't you Nonconformists be content
Sermons to make, except you preach them too?[11]

Herbert Palmer, a member of the Assembly was "highly beneficial to many by his heavenly doctrine....His speech, like that of a genuine disciple of Christ, was always with grace, with sweetness and courteous, which rendered it highly acceptable to the hearers, and well seasoned with salt."[12]

Robert Harris was a divine who knew the well-known pulpit axiom: "I preach, as if I ne'er should preach again; and, as a dying man, to dying men." This same Harris, both a Pastor and President of Trinity College, Oxford, was known for excellent order in nurturing his own children in the faith, stating this as his last will: "Also, I bequeath to all my children and their children's children, to each of them a Bible with this inscription, 'None but Christ.' "[13] His illnesses were public knowledge, and yet he found sweet delight in the Lord, accounting as his best days, those in which he "enjoyed most intercourse with Heaven." After a long testimony to the power of the fellowship of sufferings with Christ, Harris "did not expect much from any man, were his parts ever so great, until he was broken by afflictions and temptations."[14] Harris observed with a keen spiritual eye, that "it was just for God to deny us the comforts of our graces, when we deny Him the glory of them," and that "the humblest preachers converted the greatest number of souls, not the most choice scholars while unbroken."[15] It was Harris who had the insight to say, "A preacher has three books to study: the Bible, himself, and the people...that preaching to the people was but one part of the pastor's duty: he was to live and die in them, as well as for them."[16] In sickness he said, "I never in all my life saw the worth of Christ, nor tasted the sweetness of God's love, in so great a measure as I now do."

Fasts

The Assembly often fasted. At one fast, John Arrowsmith preached for an hour from Haggai 2:4, 5; and Richard Vines led in prayer for nearly two hours, followed by a second sermon which also lasted an hour. At this public fast, "Reynolds, after a short prayer, preached on 'If any man will come after me, let him deny himself.' In his concluding exhortation he exclaimed, 'Oh, that when the church is in a flame, any should come with a mind to serve their own turns by the common fire.' They should deny their own opinions rather than hinder the peace of the church....And he concluded by quoting Paul, 'Look not every man on his own things, but on the things of theirs; let the same mind be in you which was also in Christ Jesus.' "[17]

On one occasion Henry Hall led a solemn fast, just prior to the convening of the Assembly (May 29, 1643), preaching on suffering as an aid to sanctification, difficult though it be. Said Hall, "A Christian is never so glorious, as when he suffers most reproach and ignominy for Christ's sake....Keep alive this sacred fire, upon the altar of our hearts, that it may inflame our devotion toward God, kindle our love toward men, and burn out all our corruptions."[18]

The divines were not afraid to confess their sins publicly. On one occasion, "Palmer rose with the words, 'I desire to begin there,' and opened with the fault of slack attendance, coming late and going early, especially the sparse attendance at committees. It throws a curious light upon their proceedings that he said that during the meetings there was 'reading of news,' 'talking and in confusion; we do not attend at the beginning nor ending for prayer as we ought to do.' His next complaint is also a perennial one: 'On the one hand, some of us are too forward to speak, and some are, I fear too backward.' Finally, he referred to 'unhappy differences and unbeseeming phrases.' "[19]

Another aspect of spirituality was the undying commitment of these Assemblymen to the spiritual nurture of children, emphasis on family, Sabbath and character formation. As observed at the 250th anniversary of the Westminster Assembly in 1893:

> There is a most real and vital connection between belief and conduct, between creed and character. What men believe, that they become....The Westminster divines well understood the necessity of training up a child in the way he should go in order to insure against his departing from it in age. They heard and heeded the risen Master's commission to Simon Peter, "Feed my *lambs.*" Their very best work...is found in the provision which they made for the lambs of the flock....If the Westminster Assembly had done nothing more than produced the Shorter Catechism they would be entitled to the everlasting gratitude of the Christian church...next to the Bible, it was probably the best book in the world. Hence, wherever these doctrines have been received they

have brought forth the fruits of righteousness. What Dr. Chalmers said of Scotland is true the world over: "Wherever there has been most Calvinism, men have been most moral."[20]

Belief and practice were inseparable for these Westminster forefathers. The following observation was made at the 250th commemoration:

[The divines] have been criticized for being too strict and uncompromising in their views of life and duty. But all excellence is marked by strictness. Strictness certainly characterizes everything which truly represents God. The laws of nature are all strict; the laws of hygiene are strict; and the life which would secure their benediction must be a strict life. So with the laws of morals. Like him who ordained them they know "no variableness nor shadow of turning." Any pretended exposition of the moral nature and claims of God which is characterized by looseness...brands itself as false. Their narrowness has been unctuously deplored. But after all is it not the narrowness of truth? The Master himself said, "Strait is the gate and narrow is the way which leadeth unto life, and few there be that find it." "Narrowness," it has been said, "is often the badge of usefulness." Great leaders of men have been narrow. Elijah was too narrow to adopt the worship of Baal. Martin Luther was too narrow to include in his creed the errors of the Papacy. Wesley was too narrow to sympathize with the cold ritualism of his age. William Carey was so narrow that he had no sympathy with the anti-mission spirit of his age. Gideon was so narrow that he could not tolerate the idols in his father's house, but rose in the night and tore them down.[21]

One of the telltale emblems of Westminster spirituality

was a love for God's Sabbath. Most of the divines shared the sentiments of poet George Herbert (d. 1633) who spoke of the Sabbath as, "O Day most calm, most bright, the fruit of this, the next worlds bud, th'indorsement of supreme delight," and "the Sundaies of man's life, threaded together on time's string, make bracelets to adorn the wife of the eternall glorious King."[22] A historian commemorating the spiritual disciplines of the divines a hundred years ago made this correlation:

> The family and the Sabbath! The two institutions of Eden which survived the wreck of the fall! They are the two strong supports of all social order...upon which human society rests. Let them be disintegrated and social chaos inevitably follows. These two institutions our venerable Standards exalt....For their maintenance the Presbyterian Church has always stood....they have been handed down to us as a precious legacy from God-fearing ancestors. We have received them as a high trust, to be passed on in unimpaired integrity to generations yet to come. Shame upon us if they suffer loss in our hands!...These two springs of blessing have been opened for us, at unspeakable cost, by hearts and hands long stilled in death. We have drunk from them and been refreshed. But alas! the Philistines are at work to close them up with the rubbish of earth and hinder their outflow of blessing. There are no institutions of our holy religion which the great enemy of all good is attacking today with more persistent or subtle malignity and zeal. We are threatened with the dire calamity of losing the home and the Sabbath that our forefathers know.[23]

Often another true measure of one's Christian vitality is weighed at the conclusion of one's life. At his death, Jeremiah Whittaker prayed,

> O, my God, break open the prison door, and set my

poor captive soul free: but enable me to wait willingly
thy time. I desire to be dissolved. Never was any man
more desirous of life, than I am of death. When will
that time come, when I shall neither sin nor sorrow
any more?...When shall this earthly tabernacle be
dissolved, that I may be clothed upon, with that
house which is from heaven?...The soul that would
be truly wise, And taste substantial joys, Must rise
above this giddy world, And all its trifling toys. Our
treasure and heart's with God, We die to all on earth.[24]

A final attribute of this spirituality is bravery.

Courage is another trait which to a marked degree has
characterized such as are moulded by this creed. It is
not true that "conscience makes cowards of us all."
This is true only of a bad conscience. A good conscience makes a man a hero. He who walks in the fear
of God is emancipated from lower fears. He who
believes in an Almighty Father, who has foreordained
whatsoever comes to pass, and who through his
overruling providence is preserving and governing
all his creatures, and all their actions, is made superior to those experiences of life which cause others to
quake and fear. Hence, Bancroft says, "A coward and
a Puritan never went together."[25]

The Westminster assemblymen were pious men. If we'll
enjoy the perspective from this window, not only should we be
spurred on to greater faithfulness in our Christian living, but
also in our appreciation for their work. James Reid, in reflecting
on the value of familiarity with these divines, noted that in this
company we have,

a brilliant constellation...[of] sound principles, Christian dispositions, and conversation becoming the
gospel of Christ. In these, we may clearly see the

power of divine grace shining forth in all its glory in real life, subduing the inbred corruptions of our fallen nature, and animating to every good word and work. In these, we may see pious and learned men eminently zealous in the advancement of true religion, and earnestly contending for the faith which was once delivered unto the saints.[26]

Samuel Rutherford was known as an ardent defender of the faith. As he was dying, Rutherford said, "I feed upon manna, I have angels' food, my eyes shall see my Redeemer, I know that He shall stand at the latter day on the earth, and I shall be caught up in the clouds to meet Him in the air...I sleep in Christ, and when I awake I shall be satisfied with his likeness. O for arms to embrace him." His final words were "Glory, glory dwells in Emmanuel's land."

In the hymn "The Sands of Time are Sinking," Anne Cousin paraphrased the dying words of Rutherford:

O Christ, he is the fountain, the deep, sweet well of love!
The streams on earth I've tasted more deep I'll drink above:
There to an ocean fulness his mercy doth expand,
And glory, glory dwelleth in Emmanuel's land.

Questions for Review.

1. What is the biblical basis for fasting? Do you find this to be a helpful spiritual practice?

2. How well does genuine humility typify genuine piety?

3. How can willingness to confess be an indication of spirituality? How can it be abused?

4. How can Sabbath observance be an asset in modern spirituality?

5. How well did these divines practice what they preached on their deathbeds?

For Discussion.

1. Read your church's Book of Order. What does it teach about practical spirituality?

2. What is the relationship between spiritual growth and spiritual warfare, as indicated in Scripture and by the lives of these divines?

3. Can you compare the spirituality of these divines with a Christian in our own time?

Spotlight: Anthony Tuckney

Anthony Tuckney (1599–1670) was born into a minister's family in Lincolnshire, and educated at Emmanuel College, Cambridge. Following his graduation, he tutored many students who went on to play significant roles in both church and state. His first ministerial assignment was as assistant to John Cotton, minister of Boston. In 1633, John Cotton resigned his pastorate in England and went to New England, with Tuckney succeeding him as pastor.

At the Westminster Assembly, Tuckney was so respected that he served on the most important committees—the committee for examination of prospective ministers and the Committee of Accommodation—to seek to reconcile the differing views of the various parties. He also had a primary role in developing the Confession of Faith and catechisms. It is thought that many of the answers in the Larger Catechism, especially in the wording of the exposition of the Ten Commandments, are derived from his fertile mind.

He later served as Pastor of Michael-Quern church in London, and became Master of Emmanuel College in 1645, and Vice-Chancellor of the university in 1648. Tuckney had an illustrious academic career, being appointed Master of St. John's College in 1653. When urged to regard the godly in admitting students to St. Johns, he replied that he highly regarded the godly, but would admit none but scholars. For, he added, candidates could deceive him in respect to their godliness, but not as to their scholarship. He succeeded the eminent Dr. Arrowsmith as Royal Professor, while at the same time retaining his great humility. This faithful teacher took those things he had heard and passed them on to faithful students, who in turn would pass them on to others (2 Tim. 2:2).

In 1662 he was ejected with his fellow ministers in the Act of Uniformity and died in 1670 at the age of 71. He left behind a number of written works, among them a collection of 40 sermons, published posthumously (1676) and a collection of theological lectures and discourses in Latin, published in Amsterdam (1679).

Tuckney was a respected leader at the Assembly who frequently helped it move to a vote on the questions. He was an ardent Presbyterian.

10. Critics of the Assembly

Taken together, these Westminster standards consti-
tute one of the classic formulations of Reformed
theology. That so many learned and contentious men
in an age of so much theological hair-splitting could
with so little coercion establish so resounding a consensus on so detailed a doctrinal statement is one of
the marvels of the century.[1]

The Westminster Assembly has never lacked critics. At the
time it met, the Assembly's arch-critic was King Charles I,
who in response to the June 22, 1643 ordinance by Parliament
calling for the Assembly, answered with his own June 22, 1643
proclamation from Oxford forbidding and pre-annulling the
Assembly. Of the constituency of the Assembly, Charles charged
"that the far greater part of them were Men of no Reputation or
Learning, and eminently disaffected to the Government of the
Church of England, and many of them Persons who had openly
preached Rebellion, and had excited the People to take up Arms
against him, and so were not likely to be proper Instruments of
Peace and Happiness in Church or State."[2]

King Charles regarded the assemblymen as subversive,
rebellious, second-rate theologians. He viewed their very as-
sembling as unlawful (contrast this to the First Amendment of
the U.S. Constitution, which grants freedom of assembly). The
king considered that,

according to the laws of this kingdom no synod or
convocation of the clergy ought to be called but by his

authority, nor any canons or constitutions made or executed but by his Majesty's license first obtained to the making of them, and his royal assent granted to put the same in execution, on pain that every one of the clergy doing the contrary and thereof convicted suffer imprisonment and make fine to the king's will, doth strictly inhibit and forbid all and every person named in that pretended Ordinance to assemble and meet together to the end and purpose there set down, declaring further the said Assembly (if they shall convene without his Majesty's authority) to be illegal, the acts thereof not binding on his subjects, and that he will proceed severely against all those who, after such a gracious warning, shall presume to meet together by color of the said pretended Ordinance.[3]

Many of the King's loyal ministers agreed with him and became regular critics of the Assembly as did the Anglican clergy. Says Clarendon,

Of the whole number, they were not above twenty, who were not declared and avowed enemies to the doctrine or discipline of the church of England; some (many) of them infamous in their lives and conversations; and most of them of very mean parts in learning, if not of scandalous ignorance; and of no other reputation, than of malice to the church of England; so that that convention has not since produced anything that might not then reasonably have been expected from it.[4]

While one might agree with Clarendon that many of the assemblymen were avowed enemies of episcopacy, the claim that they were not well-educated is wrong, when one considers how many were educated at Cambridge (68) and Oxford (48).

Some critics complained that the makeup of the Assembly

was not the best England could offer. John Milton even accused Parliament of nominating certain assemblymen, with political motive. However, Thomas Fuller says that Parliament "thought it not fit to entrust the clergy with their own choice, of whose general corruption they constantly complained; and therefore adjudged it unfit that the distempered patients should be, or choose their own physicians."[5]

An Assembly contemporary, Richard Baxter (who did not agree with the divines on everything) said: "They were men of eminent learning, godliness, and ministerial abilities and fidelity. And being not worthy to be one of them myself, I may more fully speak the truth, which I know, even in the face of malice and envy. That as far as I am able to judge, by the information of history, and by any other evidences, the Christian world, since the days of the apostles, had never a synod of more excellent divines, than this synod, and the synod of Dordt."[6]

Religious Critics

Two of the most vocal critics of the Assembly were the Roman Catholics and the Anglicans. The Romanist church had been a quarry of criticism for Protestantism for more than a century. Specifically, Romanists disdained the Protestant emphasis on the clarity of Scripture to the common person, the sufficiency of Christ's work, and the equality of believers in the Lord.

Anglicans were theological, as well as political, critics; especially when the Westminster divines called for the abolition of bishops, disagreed with some aspects of the Anglican sacraments and advocated a Reformed worship. In his *Remarks on the History of Scotland*, Judge Hailles says:

It cannot be expected, indeed, that royalists and high churchmen, especially such as were involved in the disputes of the times, would give a favorable character to an assembly whose sentiments were so entirely opposed to their own. But in the judgment of all orthodox, evangelical theologians, there has, from the first, been but one opinion; and that is, that probably, since the days of the apostles, a more learned, judicious, and pious assembly of divines has never been convened.[7]

Another religious group intensely critical of Westminster were the Arminians, who could not endure the concept of the sole sovereignty of God. On topics like election, predestination, and the definition of the church in terms of the elect, nearly any mention of God's will trumping man's will sent Arminians into a frenzy of criticism. There were many Arminians in the Anglican leadership at the time of the Assembly.

Other Puritan groups were also critical of the divines and their works. Independents like Goodwin, Nye and Burroughs (not to mention Owen and Baxter who were not present) sided with the Westminster Presbyterians in many questions. These two groups were allied in their commitment to Scripture and their rejection of hierarchical forms and formal worship. However, at the Assembly, they discovered several areas of disagreement. The Independents found themselves (perhaps even regretfully) critical of the Assembly's views on government. In their *Apologeticall Narration* the Independents noted that the Assembly consisted of "many able, learned, and grave divines, where much of the piety, wisdom, and learning of the two kingdoms met in one."[8] However, this work contained a severe criticism of the Westminster structures for church government—basically the Assembly leaned toward Presbyterian government.

Some caricatured the Assembly as intolerant. This criticism plagued the Assembly for years. John Birkenhead (1616–1679), in his 1647 burlesque, *The Assembly-Man*, illustrates the accusation of the divines for intolerance: "The onely difference 'twixt the Assembler and a Turk, is, that one plants Religion by the power of the Sword, and the other by the power of the scimitar." He proceeded to allege, "Nay, the greatest strife in their whole Conventicle, is who shall do worst; for they all intend to make the Church but a Sepulchre, having not onely plundered, but anatomized all the true Clergy."[9]

The divines were frequently accused of having the desire to seize power to persecute their opponents. Fairborn alleges that "to the Presbyterians, toleration was the very man of sin" and Masson, Milton's biographer, accused the Assembly: "Toleration to them was a demon, a chimera, the Great Diana of the Independents."[10] Yet in response, Hetherington wisely counters that "both the principles and the constitution of a rightly formed Presbyterian Church render the usurpation of power and the exercise of tyranny on its part wholly impossible."

What they did assert, in common with virtually all Christians of their age, whether Roman Catholic or Protestant, was that error should not be allowed to propagate itself freely. They held that the church should identify error as such and that the Christian civil magistrate (where there was one) should take measures to ensure suppression of those seeking to spread it. To the extent that this is intolerance, with virtually all others of their time, they were intolerant. (Roman Catholics, of course, went much further in that they punished—even burned alive—those simply suspected of holding erroneous views.)

They were also accused of immoderation in seeking to elucidate so many biblical truths. However, the Confession of Faith is quite moderate and non-inventive in its formulation of biblical truth. An example of the Assembly's moderation is that it did not seek to settle the speculative controversy about the order of God's decrees in salvation, instead leaving those debatable matters to the academics. Although the moderator, Twisse, had well-formed opinions on this subject, such specificity did not make it into the WCF. Rather than taking particular positions on every subject, the Assembly only spoke on those matters on which the Bible speaks clearly, and on which they consequently believed everyone fit to be officers in the church would agree as a confession of their faith as well. Doubtful matters were not included. The WCF does not lay out an elaborate end-time scheme, nor treat complex ethical issues. Neither does it attempt to settle all conceivable issues. It is restrained and moderate in scope.

Personal Critics

John Milton, a leading Elizabethan poet, at first was very favorable in his comments about the Assembly, but became critical after its views on divorce were formed (he had recently divorced his wife). In 1646 in his sonnet, "On the New Forcers of Conscience Under the Long Parliament," Milton accused the Presbyterians of seeking to forcibly impose their views on others. Milton rhymingly alleged:

> Your plots and packing, worse than those of Trent,
>   that so the Parliament
> May with their wholesome and preventive shears
> Clip your phylacteries, though baulk your ears, and
>   succour our just fears
> When they shall read this clearly in your charge: New
>   *Presbyter* is but old Priest writ large.

In his *Fragments of a History of England*, Milton said:

And if the state were in this plight, religion was not in a much better, to reform which a certain number of divines were called, neither chosen by any rule nor custom, ecclesiastical nor eminent for either knowledge or piety above others left out; only as each member of Parliament, in his private fancy thought fit, so elected one by one. The most of them were such as had preached or cried down, with great show of zeal, the avarice and pluralities of bishops and prelates....Yet these conscientious men, (ere any part of the work was done for which they came together, and that on the public salary) wanted not boldness to the ignominy and scandal of their pastorlike profession, and especially of their boasted reformation—to seize into their hands, or not unwillingly to accept, besides one, two or more of the best livings—such as collegiate masterships in the university, rich livings in the city; setting sail to all winds that might blow gain into their covetous bosoms....So that between the teachers, and these the disciples, there hath not been a more ignominious and mortal wound to faith, to piety, to the work of reformation; nor more cause of blaspheming given to the enemies of God and truth, since the first preaching of the reformation.[11]

Milton even roasted the divines in his most famous epic poem, *Paradise Lost*. One scene was based on the sitting of the Assembly, as angry Milton compared the divines to the fallen angels in the infernal world. Milton likely had the Assembly in mind when he wrote:

Others, apart, sat on a hill retired,
In thought more elevate, and reasoned high
Of Providence, foreknowledge, will and fate;
Fixed fate, free will, foreknowledge absolute;
And found no end, in wandering mazes lost.[12]

Other doggerels mocking the Assembly were composed as well, for example:

Pretty Synod doth it sit,
Void of grace, as well of wit,
    And make no canons;
But such as ordinance are called,

Which have the very souls enthralled
Of every man own's.

Now from black Tom and Blacker Noll,
That kill and flay without control,
   Thereby to end us;
From Synod's nonsense and their treason,
And from their catechistic reason,
   Good heaven, defend us![13]

It seems as if during the Restoration, the composing of doggerel satirizing aspects of the Assembly rose to an art form. In one well-known ridicule of the Assembly, *Hudibras*, Samuel Butler charged,

A vile Assembly 'tis, that can
No more be prov'd by Scripture, than
Provincial, Classick, National,
Mere human Creature-Cobwebs all.[14]

Later still, in his rejection of the Assembly's view of government as derived from Scripture (divine-right), Butler mocks,

Of Church-Rule, and by Right Divine.
Bel and the Dragon's [an apocryphal book] Chaplains were
More moderate than these by far:
For they (poor knaves) were glad to cheat,
To get their Wives and Children Meat;
But these will not be sobb'd off so,
They must have Wealth and Power too;
Or else with Blood and Desolation
They'll tear it out o' th' Heart o' th' Nation.[15]

And commenting on this, Zachary Grey noted, "The great gorbelly'd Idol called the Assembly of Divines is not ashamed in this time of State Necessity, to guzzle down, and devour daily more at an ordinary Meal, than would make a Feast of *Bel and the Dragon*: For besides their fat Benefices [stipend] forsooth, they must have their Four Shillings a Day for sitting in Constollidation."[16]

One of the most stinging critics of the Assembly was Royalist sympathizer John Birkenhead whose *The Assembly-Man*, contained some of the bitterest scorn for the Assembly. Birkenhead charged that the divines were chosen according to the criteria of those who "knew least of all his Profession," and alleged that they sat "four years towards a new Religion, but in the interim left none at all."[17] Moreover, he esteemed the divines as "Atoms; petty small Levites, whose parts are not perceptible," and as those who "follow the Geneva Margin, as those Seamen who understand not the Compass crept along the shore."[18]

Birkenhead, the critic, valued the Shorter Catechism as "paultry"; accused the divines of being materially motivated, only interested in "silver chains"; and satirized that "though the Assembler's Brains are Lead, his Countenance is Brass; for he condemned such as held two Benefices, while he himself has four or five, besides his Concubin-Lecture."[19] Barbs were fired at individual assemblymen as well. This example was aimed at an eminent Professor of Theology at Cambridge: "So that Learning now is so much advanced, as Arrowsmith's Glass-eye sees more than his Natural."[20]

The Puritan traits of the divines are mocked: "[A divine's] two longest things are his Nails and his Prayer. But the cleanest thing about him is his Pulpit cushion, for he still beats the dust out of it."[21] Of the Puritan long-windedness, Birkenhead ridicules a divine, "Yet though you heard him three hours, he'll ask a fourth....If he has got any new Tale or Expression, 'tis easier to make Stones speak than him to hold his peace. He hates a Church where there is an Echo for it robs him of his dear Repetition, and confounds the Auditory as well as he," and of their sermons, "had they the art to shorten it into Sense, they might write his whole Sermon on the back of their Nail."[22]

Criticisms often tagged the divines as dupes of Parliament: "At Fasts and Thanksgivings the Assembler is the States' Trumpet; for then he doth not preach, but is blown; proclaim News, very loud, the Trumpet and his Forehead both of one metal."[23]

The divines also had their bravery challenged: "Before a Battle the Assembly ever speaks to the Soldiers; and the holding up of his hands must be as necessary as Moses's against the Amalekites: For he pricks them on, tells them that God loves none but the valiant: but when Bullets fly, himself turns first, and then cries 'All the sons of Adam are cowards!'…being wise as a Sheep and innocent as a Wolf."[24]

Birkenhead's summation of the character of the divines is that they have "the Pride of three Tyrants, the Forehead of six Gaolers, and the Fraud of twelve Brokers. Or take him in the Bunch, and their whole Assembly is a Club of Hypocrites, where six dozen schismatics spend two hours for four shillings apiece."[25]

Episcopalians, Erastians and Cromwell charged that the Assembly, "did cry down the truth with votes, and was an anti-Christian meeting which would erect a Presbytery worse than Bishops."[26]

Modern Critics

There has been a long history of criticism of the Assembly, and it has not abated. One reason to hear the critics of the Assembly as fully as we have, is to see that errors haven't changed much in some respects. In terms of basic ideas, the opponents of Westminster 350 years ago are still with us today. In fact, if anything, they have multiplied.

Sadly, through the centuries, the thought and personnel of this Assembly have been scandalized. Critics have not been satisfied merely to debate the contribution of this Assembly, moreover they have vandalized the reputation of these divines. Rocks have been thrown through this window. As we look on from the courtyard, we see broken windows, graffiti on stone walls, and an overgrown courtyard. Rummaging through the rubble, however, we see that even the most severe critics have not so much tarnished the work of the Assembly, as revealed their own biases.

The civil critics of Westminster, usually focus on what they see as the intolerance of the divines. Many moderns read these Westminster documents and find a rather uncompromising view of the role of civil government. The original wording of the WCF assigned the task of supporting the truths of Scripture to the civil government. In our culture, that is not allowed, lest it violate the separation between church and state. In that the original versions of the WCF allowed the state more religious sponsorship, this was interpreted by critics as an attempt to force the Christian faith on others. Of course, the WCF itself did not recommend this, but just a positive support of the true church and a suppression of the propagation of error. (Note the difference between punishing those who hold erroneous beliefs, as did Roman Catholicism, and curtailing its spread, the position of the Assembly.) The Assembly expected the civil magistrate, when a Christian, to do this. Still the critics love to misrepresent the Assembly and to heave this rock through a window.

The religious critics of the Assembly are still all those who are anti-Calvinists in one form or another. To this day, one will meet no Roman Catholics who are fond of the WCF. On several grounds, Romanists are highly critical of the Westminster formulations. They object to the teaching on predestination, the finished work of Christ, the non-necessity of human priesthood, the sacraments and government. Roman Catholics, like most other critics, do not reject individual aspects of the Westminster faith, but rather the whole system.

Most other hierarchical groups still criticize the Westminster system. Episcopalians, Methodists, and other churches with a pyramid-shaped leadership, do not agree with the government espoused by the divines. On the other hand, Independents strongly disagree with the connectional nature of government, and the required submission to the higher governing bodies.

Another strain among many evangelical independents today (which was not present in the independents 350 years ago), is a strong disagreement with the WCF's teaching on the unity of the covenant. A large sector of evangelical Christianity believes that God works differently in different eras of time, and thus rejects the seventh chapter of the WCF. In addition, this dispensation-based approach to the Bible sees a lasting separation between ethnic Israel and the church. That, too, is a cause for some to criticize and reject the WCF.

Still by far, the largest group of professing Christians who criticize the work of this Assembly are spiritual children of Jacob Arminius (1560–1609). This man, who studied under one of Calvin's disciples, returned to Holland in the late sixteenth century, and sought to modify the Reformed faith. He was tried in Holland, and found to have strayed from the Reformation teaching in a number of subjects. He taught that humans themselves chose to follow God, that they could lose salvation (or fall from grace), that God only elected based on what he saw ahead of time that people would choose anyway, and that Christ's death had an effect even on the unsaved.

One of his leading followers was John Wesley, the founder of Methodism, who has influenced so many. Wesley and others helped popularize Arminius' message, and today have millions of followers. This family of Christians strenuously object to the teachings of the historic Reformation faith. They do not merely disagree with one of two particulars of the WCF, but are critical of the entire system.

Another large segment frequently critical of this Assembly is the anti-creedal set. Many of us have heard people say, "No creed, but Christ; no book, but the Bible." While that is a catchy jingle, it can hardly be defended. Many critics have thrown stones at the work of the Assembly, because it produced a systematic assortment of biblical summaries. Some wrongly believe that any systematizing kills the spirit, as if consistency (say in issuing paychecks, or in the timing of meals) is, in and of itself, evil. Critics of Westminster who oppose any creed would do well to compare the WCF with Scripture before they repudiate it.

There really is only one new religious critic of the Assembly—that new breed of professing Christian who is far too wise and modern to stoop to the unenlightened ignorance expressed 350 years ago.

These modernists come in several varieties. One is the liberal Presbyterian, who has forsaken the historic expressions of the truths illuminated at Westminster. Since the last commemoration of the Assembly in 1943, many Presbyterian denominations have even ceased using the WCF as the doctrinal standard for their church. Many liberal Presbyterians now scoff at these "ancient paths" (cf. Jer. 6:16), and mock these teachings as the babbling of a pre-scientific group of unenlightened people. Many modern Presbyterians value pluralism over biblical truth, and emotional inclusion over biblical exclusion. These liberal Presbyterians no longer associate themselves with Westminster, and have joined the stone-throwers in the past century, now rejecting the Westminster summaries. Few of these will even recall the anniversary of this event, having joined the ranks of critics.

Another modern critic is the liberal evangelical. This evangelical holds to the same underlying pluralism that will not allow him to adhere to any confession of fixed truth. He has elevated feeling and acceptability over some of the hard (and often unpopular) biblical realities contained in the WCF.

Other modern critics are those who may even celebrate Westminster commemorations with us, but who have hearts that are far from the sentiments of the divines. They have a pharisaic Presbyterianism that wears the outer garb; they may even go to a "Presbyterian" church; but they do not hold to the values of the WCF. These, too, see themselves as superior to our grandfathers of the faith. These modernists also join in with those who pelt the windows of Westminster with stones of rejection. Many value openness and modernity more than historic truth.

C. S. Lewis once gave an apt reply to critics who encouraged excessive openness of mind. For all those who wanted our minds flung open as wide as the horizons, with no barriers of fixed truth, Lewis retorted: "An open mind, in questions that are not ultimate, is useful. But an open mind about ultimate foundations...is idiocy. If a man's mind is open on these things, let his mouth at least be shut."[27]

Questions for Review.

1. How do you react to valid criticisms? Can criticism be constructive? Share a few examples.

2. How can criticism help strengthen a group or individuals? Do our assemblies benefit or suffer from criticism?

3. What were the main criticisms of Westminster by (a) Roman Catholics, (b) Anglicans, and (c) Independents? What new groups today are critical of the work of Westminster? Why?

4. From your knowledge of the WCF, is it intolerant or moderate? How would you characterize it?

5. When we make criticisms, how can we also avoid violating the ninth commandment ("You shall not give false testimony")? Can you speak the truth in love in criticism?

For Discussion.

1. What are some of the dangers when the church is too closely aligned with political rulers?

2. In your experience, how are disciples of Westminster most often criticized? Evaluate.

3. In what areas do you think the work of Westminster is deserving of criticism?

Spotlight: Edmund Calamy

Edmund Calamy (1600–1666), born in London, graduated with his Bachelor of Divinity from Cambridge in 1632, where he inclined to the anti-Arminian party. He studied 16 hours a day, particularly mastering the controversy with the great Roman Catholic theologian Bellarmine and the works of the medieval scholastics, and was said to have read Augustine's works five times.

However, when he preached, he used plain language. He much preferred the reading of Holy Scriptures to any other works. Mr. Calamy was chosen to serve as a lecturer at Bury St. Edmunds in Suffolk County, laboring alongside Jeremiah Burroughs. In 1639 he became the Minister of Mary Aldermanbury in London and, in 1641, joined with four others (who would eventually become members of the Westminster Assembly) to author a famous tract attacking the liturgy and episcopacy of the Anglican Church as being incongruous with biblical Presbyterianism. This book was published with the authors identified as "Smectymnuus," an acronym for the first letters of their names: Stephen Marshall, Edmund Calamy, Thomas Young, Matthew Newcomen and William Spurstow. This treatise advocated the parity of bishops and presbyters in Scripture, as well as the ancient institution of ruling elders in the church. It also pointed out that the episcopal form of government was a serious departure from biblical rule.

Calamy gained a shining reputation in London, where he was "eminently distinguished by his intrepid integrity, ministerial faithfulness, solid learning, and genuine piety. He made vigorous efforts, for the progress of useful knowledge among mankind, in overthrowing error, and in defending and propagating truth." When many Irish Protestants received difficult treatment at the hands of the Roman Catholic Church, Calamy's church took up a very liberal collection to assist them, thus continuing the apostolic practice of being concerned for those in distress (Gal. 2:10).

Calamy was an eager advocate for the divine institution of ruling elder and among the first to declare before Parliament that bishop and presbyter were one. He was also one of the more popular preachers in London and a frequent preacher before the Long Parliament. Toward the end of his ministry, Calamy was removed from his pulpit at Aldermanbury by the 1662 Act of Uniformity, which required obedience to state-imposed forms and unbiblical rituals.

Offered a position as a bishop, Calamy was unable, in good conscience, to accept. Later in life, Calamy was imprisoned briefly in Newgate for preaching contrary to the Act of Uniformity. He died in October, 1666, shortly after the Great Fire.

Much of Calamy's thought is preserved in the 1654 *Jus Divinum* (a joint composition on church government), a number of his sermons, and the posthumous *The Art of Divine Meditation* (1680). Perhaps one of his greatest legacies was his eldest son, who also was one of the ministers ejected by the Act of Uniformity. His grandson was also a dissenting (a non-conformist to that state-imposed religion) divine of great eminence. Calamy was a shining example of the faith which, rejecting this world's favors, regards disgrace for the sake of Christ as of greater value than the treasures of Egypt (Heb. 11:25).

11. Why Remember?

The end of this anniversary is not self-glorification
and an ostentatious parade of denominationalism.
Nay, God's hand is in it, and it means remembrance,
stimulus, inspiration, life from the dead, and a glorious flood of light on some of the dark problems of
history.[1]

Like the events enshrined by a family as anchors of their
history, the events that a church commemorates are clues to
its self-identity. The strength of commitment to those underlying traditions is observed when a church continues those cel-
ebrations, even during times of difficulty and opposition. A
brief look at previous commemorations may help in appreciat-
ing that legacy, as well as give us guidance for the future.

Past Commemorations

The strength of commitment that American Presbyterian
churches have had to Westminster is noticeable from the first
several commemorations. The first commemoration of the
Westminster era was observed shortly after the first major
rupture in American Presbyterianism. In 1842 presbyteries
began calling for a bicentennial commemoration of the
Westminster Assembly. Remembering was a mode of Christian
education and discipleship. William Symington, a Scottish Reformed Presbyterian, helps capture the significance of the bicentennial commemoration:

We would not be chargeable with the enormous wickedness of forgetting that men are only what God makes them, and that to Him all the glory...is to be ascribed. But we are, at the same time, unable to see wherein the bestowment of a due meed of praise on the memory of such...contravenes any maxim of sound morality, or any dictate of inspiration. We...have no hesitation in attempting to awaken, in the men of the present generation, sentiments of admiration and gratitude for the memory of worthies to whom all are so deeply indebted....While we claim and exercise the right of bringing these, like all other human productions, to the infallible touchstone of Revelation...we cannot but cherish the hope that the present commemoration...may be regarded as symptomatic at once of a growing attachment to the sentiments of the Westminster divines, and of an enlightened determination to maintain them more firmly and diffuse them more extensively than ever.[2]

Thomas Smyth stated the value of commemoration in this fashion:

If the preparation of standards which have served as bulwarks to the truth as it is in Jesus, when error and heresy have come in like a flood upon the church, and which are at this moment venerated, as containing the system of doctrine taught in the word of God, by growing multitudes; and if a devotion to the cause of human rights which no bribery or persecution could extinguish; if, I say, these achievements are sufficient to demand our gratitude, then are we imperatively called upon to hail with exultation this natal day of our spiritual birthright, to consider the days of old and the years of ancient times, and to bring to remembrance the Westminster Assembly.[3]

The Presbyterian church in 1843 expressed this value on the historical recollection of the Westminster Assembly:

> A correct knowledge of the character of that (sic) Assembly, of the purpose for which they were convened, of the difficulties of their position, of the arduous nature of their task, and of the result of their labors, how the extent of the benefits which they have conferred on the interest of truth and freedom; and our Church in common with other Churches, which have been formed on the same model, must feel that the concurrence of the Two Hundredth Anniversary of their meeting, is a deeply interesting period in the lapse of time, and may prove profitable by its appropriate commemoration.[4]

Hetherington, at the two-century mark, expressed his admiration for the chief product of the Assembly, the Confession of Faith:

> The existence of a Confession of Faith is ever a standing defense against the danger of any Church lapsing unawares into heresy….Nothing essential is omitted [from the WCF]; and nothing is extended to a length disproportioned to its due importance….It contains the calm and settled judgment of these profound divines on all previous heresies and subjects of controversy which had in any age or country agitated the Church….Each error is condemned, not by a direct statement and refutation of it, but by a clear, definite, and strong statement of the converse truth. There was, in this mode of exhibiting the truth, singular wisdom combined with equally singular modesty. Every thing of an irritating nature is suppressed, and the pure and simple truth alone displayed; while there is not only no ostentatious parade of superior learning, but even a concealment of learning.[5]

Nineteenth century commemorants were in good biblical company. As David, "the man after God's own heart," meditates, he remembers the past, the "days of long ago" (Ps. 143:5). Listen to the pledge of the exiled Israelites: "May my right hand forget its skill. May my tongue cling to the roof of my mouth if I do not remember you, if I do not consider Jerusalem my highest joy" (Ps. 137:5, 6). Clearly, remembering God's past providence was a norm and benefit for the covenant people. It was an aid for spiritual growth and perseverance.

As nearly synonymous with "trust," Psalm 20:7 (KJV) contrasts parallels: "Some trust in chariots, and some in horses; but we will remember the name of the Lord our God." In the last day, "all the ends of the earth will remember and turn to the Lord" (Ps. 22:27). Asaph, while interceding for God's help pleads, "Remember the people you purchased of old" (Ps. 74:2), and pledges, "I will remember the deeds of the Lord; yes, I will remember your miracles of long ago" (Ps. 77:11). Remembering how the Lord worked previously is, in the arsenal of the faithful, a fine weapon which we ignore at our own peril.

The next opportunity for commemoration saw the Presbyterian church divided along geographic lines. Both Northern and Southern Presbyterian churches hosted well-received and superbly planned commemoratives at the close of the nineteenth century, in 1897 and 1898 respectively.

At the 250th commemoration the participants were called on to remember, as in Hebrews 12:1–3, "that vast star-reaching amphitheater of shining immortals over looking down upon the church…the shadow of a vaster presence…[to] utilize the heroism of illustrious examples, the achievements of conquering faith, and the ravishing glory of the victor-crowned host to animate and quicken the sacramental host on earth until the end of time."[6]

Toward the end of the nineteenth century, B. B. Warfield,

a defender of the lasting value of the Westminster standards, noted:

> The significance of the Westminster Standards as a creed is to be found in the three facts that, historically speaking, they are the final crystallization of the elements of evangelical religion, after the conflicts of sixteen hundred years; scientifically speaking, they are the richest and most precise and best guarded statement ever penned of all that enters into evangelical religion and of all that must be safeguarded if evangelical religion is to persist in the world; and, religiously speaking, they are a notable monument of spiritual religion.[7]

At this same commemoration, W. G. T. Shedd reflected: "In these struggles...the gem of the gospel was cut and polished, and it is on this account that the enunciation of the gospel in the Reformed Confessions attains its highest purity, and that among other Reformed Confessions the Westminster Confession, the product of the Puritan conflict, reaches a perfection of statement never elsewhere achieved."[8]

The 1897 Assembly of the PCUS, meeting in Charlotte, N.C., was treated to a true feast, the committee having done an excellent job of preparation. The following were the topics: (1) the social and political background of the Assembly; (2) the religious situation of Britain at the time; (3) a description of the Assembly, its personnel, proceedings, and place of meeting; (4) the doctrinal contents of the Confession; (5) the nature, value, and utility of the Catechisms; (6) the polity and worship of the Westminster standards; (7) the present relations among those churches which hold the Westminster symbols; (8) the influence of the Westminster symbols on missionary activity; (9) the relation of the Westminster standards to current theology and the needs of the future; (10) the influence of the Westminster symbols on family and society; and (11) the influence of

Westminster on civil liberty and government.

The 1897 Southern commemoration concluded by recording the value of commemorations:

> With God's blessing upon these celebrations, good
> will surely will follow. Larger knowledge of the ori-
> gin and contents of our Standards will be one result.
> Greater devotion to the system of doctrine, polity,
> and worship which they contain will surely be kindled.
> And a renewed purpose to spread these great teach-
> ings abroad among men will no doubt be formed by
> many of our people. A revived interest in the doc-
> trines of the Reformed system will be the sure result,
> and with this will come vigorous spiritual life and
> quickened religious activity in the conquest of the
> world for the Lord Jesus Christ.[9]

Not a mere historical or ecclesiastical exercise, this celebration was intended to aid the spiritual interest, vitality and
activity of churches and individuals.

Of the value of the 1897 and other commemorations, one
participant wrote:

> There is a great moral element. Sometimes it is good
> to get free from the narrow environments of the
> immediate present and ascend some eminence which
> commands a view of ways long since trodden, and
> then, from what is taught in the review, learn to
> forecast the ever-widening way of the future. It is
> only by such studies that we catch the spirit of the
> great historic eras which have been potent in shaping
> the institutions of our own times. It is only when we
> can transport ourselves to the distant past and evoke
> from its obscurity the forms of its heroic men; it is only
> when we acquaint ourselves with the errors they

combated, the difficulties they surmounted, the hard-
ships they endured, that we can fully comprehend the
character of the men who thus toiled and suffered, or
appreciate the value.[10]

In 1943, embroiled in WWII, American churches did not
turn their primary attention to commemoration of the Assembly. (At these commemorations there were six addresses as
compared with 23 at the 1897–1898 commemorations.) On
Sunday May 30, 1943, one day before the Southern Presbyterian
celebration, the Assembly met in the Masonic Auditorium in
Detroit with a commemorative celebration which included
addresses by Dr. J. Harry Cotton ("The Sovereign God and
Human Liberties") and Dr. Edward Howell Roberts ("Faith of
our Fathers"). In his message addressed to youth, Roberts
contended: "A very penetrating thinker has observed, 'When
you hear anyone say, "Away with creeds," you know that what
he really means is "take mine." ' Everyone has a creed. There is
not a single exception. And we live according to what we really
believe. How foolish then the prejudice against doctrine. Much
of it is based upon ignorance."[11]

To further assist in celebration of this Tercentenary, which
was to be held on Reformation Sunday (Oct. 31) 1943, every
active pastor, seminary professor and chaplain received a packet
containing a brochure with a historical sketch of the Assembly,
a description of the documents created, and an essay on the
abiding values of the Assembly's work; a suggested order of
worship; an announcement of a Tercentenary Sermon Contest;
a bibliography of relevant books handled by Presbyterian book-
stores; samples of church calendars for the month of October;
and a folder with suggestions for celebration. This occasion was
also the first attempt at a commemorative radio hookup, as the
PCUSA arranged with CBS for a nationwide broadcast of
Moderator Henry Sloane Coffin's address.

1993 and Beyond

Twentieth century commemorations began to show a doctrinal slide. By the end of the twentieth century, the geographic division of North and South had healed, although a broader theological divide was evident. At the 350th anniversary of the convening of the Assembly, the largest American Presbyterian church (the PCUSA) observed no celebration of the WCF. This was understandable, both because of their multi-confessional approach, and because the specifics of the WCF were no longer the stated beliefs of many of their members.

The only remaining American celebrants were those from churches that had abandoned the mainline churches. These groups, for the first time, gathered together for a transdenominational celebration in September 1993, in London. The speakers and topics were: James M. Boice, "The Sovereignty of God"; William S. Barker, "The Men and Parties of the Assembly"; John R. de Witt, "The Form of Church Government"; Samuel T. Logan, Jr., "The Seating and Work of the Assembly"; Wayne Spear, "The Westminster Confession of Faith and Holy Scripture"; Douglas F. Kelly, "The Westminster Shorter Catechism"; Robert Godfrey, "The Westminster Larger Catechism"; Joel Nederhood, "The Preeminence of Christ"; Iain Murray, "The Directory for Public Worship"; Robert M. Norris, "The Preaching of the Assembly"; Jay E. Adams, "The Influence of Westminster"; and Eric Alexander, "The Application of Redemption."

The 1993 celebration was not only interdenominational, but international. The question on the minds of participants was, Would it be the climactic, final peak, or the beginning of a new resurgence of the Westminster communions? By the next half century, would the Westminster faith grow among its own family members, or shrink as it had among the mainline participants? Would Presbyterians even have a 400th anniversary of the Assembly? If not, it was also likely that the Westminster brand of Presbyterianism would not exist, so basic were the standards to its heart.

If there was a 400th anniversary commemoration, would it be conducted out of memory, or just out of nostalgia? Cultural critic Christopher Lasch has suggested that an awareness of the difference between nostalgia and memory can help ward off falling prey to various idolatries. Lasch warned that if any type of recollection of the past does not employ an intelligent eye toward the future, as well, then the "ideological twin" of proper memory, nostalgia, "undermines the ability to make intelligent use of the past. Memory, in contrast, does not idealize the past to condemn the present, but draws hope from the past in order to enrich the present and guide the future."[12] In any commemoration, we would be prudent to mark well this distinction.

When people do not remember the Lord and his past workings, consequences are dire. For example, when Israel did not remember the Lord in Judges 8:34, or when Joash did not remember the Lord's kindness (2 Chron. 24:22), or when "there was no remembrance of men of old" (Eccles. 1:11), these were indications of low-level faith. Solomon bemoans the loss of memory of the things of old and also recognizes that when one generation loses that asset in the arsenal of faith, "even those who are yet to come will not be remembered by those who follow" (Eccles. 1:11). And this spiritual amnesia is not a virtue, as if "Old is mold and New is true." In an age of cultural and spiritual decline, wise men of old are not remembered (Eccles. 2:16). Along with this comes a callousness that results in the poor not being remembered (Eccles. 9:15; cf. also Paul's injunction to remember the poor in Gal. 2:10). Could it be that insensitivity to the poor and to those around us is related to the loss of remembering what God has done in the past? Biblical authors seemed to suggest that our appreciation of God's whole counsel as exhibited in the past is intimately bound with present obedience to that all-encompassing counsel. The loss of proper commemoration, may indeed lead to the loss of extending the

Lordship of Christ in all areas of life. As George Grant has written,

> History is not just the concern of historians and social scientists. It is not the lonely domain of political prognosticators and ivory tower academics. It is the very stuff of life. And, it is the very stuff of faith. In fact, the Bible puts a heavy emphasis on historical awareness....Again and again in the Scriptures, God calls upon His people to remember....He calls on us to remember the splendor, strength, and devotion of the Davidic Kingdom....He calls on us to remember the valor, forthrightness, and holiness of the prophets (Jas 5:7–11). He calls on us to remember the glories of creation (Ps. 104:1–30), the devastation of the flood (2 Pet. 2:4–11), the judgment of the great apostasies (Jude 5–11)...the sanctity of the Lords' Day...and the ultimate victory of the cross.[13]

Perhaps in this present commemoration, as we face ebbing and flowing tides of human thought, we can share the sentiments expressed by Samuel Smith, 100 years ago:

> No other system has the inherent force to resist this rising tide as the Westminster has; it stands, therefore, today invested with an importance perhaps transcending all present possible appreciation, for should this new theology win the day there is danger that the world may be ultimately orphaned of its God as it is fast being robbed of its Bible. The part, then, that Calvinistic theology must play in the needs of the future is that of a granite ledge against the insidious encroachments of a troubled sea casting up mire and dirt; its office is to say, with the voice of that God, whose humble mouth-piece it has been privileged to prove in many a stormy period of the past, "Hitherto shalt thou come, but no further: and here shall thy

proud waves be stayed."[14]

William Symington assessed the utility of proper remembering in 1843:

> The disposition to commemorate events, whether of public or private interest, springs from a law of our nature....The very act of reminiscence itself is calculated to call into operation, and consequently to improve by exercising, some of the higher moral principles of the heart, such as gratitude for benefits received, veneration for departed worth, and imitation of praiseworthy excellence. And, even if no other advantage accrued, it might be deemed sufficient to encourage to engage in such an exercise, that it tends directly to remind us of the lapse of time—of the steady progression of those quickly-revolving cycles which are hastening on the secrets of futurity to their complete and final development; and by leading us to contemplate what has been happily called "the funeral procession of centuries," to bring us to reflect at once on "the handbreadth of our own earthly career," and on "the vast gulf of duration beyond."[15]

Winston Churchill spoke of the role of history in helping for the future: "The greatest advances in human civilization have come when we recovered what we had lost; when we learned the lessons of history."[16] And Alexander Solzhenitsyn remarked about the necessity of remembering: "To destroy a people you must first sever their roots."[17] Another insightful commentator said, "The first step in liquidating a people is to erase its memory. Destroy its books, its culture, and its history; before long the community will forget what it is, and what it was."[18] This amnesia can fall on the church, too, if it doesn't actively remember how God has worked in their life in the past.

Since the Westminster Assembly was set in Britain, it

might be appropriate to conclude with the thoughts of two British Christians, one modern, and one from the past. Frances Young observes in *The Making of Creeds:*

> Christianity is the only major religion to set such store by creeds and doctrines. Other religions have scriptures, others have their characteristic ways of worship, others have their own peculiar ethics and lifestyle; other religions also have philosophical, intellectual or mystical form as well as more popular manifestations. But except in response to Christianity, they have not developed creeds, statements of standard belief to which the orthodox are supposed to adhere. Other religions have hymns and prayers, they have festivals, they have popular myths, stories of saints and heroes, they have art forms, and have moulded whole societies and cultures. But they have no "orthodoxy," a sense of right belief which is doctrinally sound and from which deviation means heresy.[19]

And G. K. Chesterton expressed the continuing necessity of maintaining our anchors in the faith. He compared the maintenance of truth to repainting an important landmark:

> If you leave a thing alone you leave it to a torrent of change. If you leave a white post alone it will soon be a black post. If you particularly want it to be white you must be always painting it again; that is, you must be always having a revolution. Briefly, if you want the old white post you must have a new white post. But this which is true even of inanimate things is in a quite special and terrible sense true of all human things. An almost unnatural vigilance is really required of the citizen because of the horrible rapidity with which human institutions grow old.[20]

Another historian noted: "History is the handmaid of

Providence, the priestess of truth, and the mother of wisdom. And if our indebtedness to the past is at all times a profitable theme for meditation, surely there are few [occasions] at which one can more easily or more delightfully put himself under the inspiration and the sanctity of the great communion of the faithful of bygone days."[21]

We Christians must hold fast to what we've been taught. As Hebrews 10:23 says, "Let us hold unswervingly to the hope we profess." It is not only appropriate, but also imperative for us to renew our commitment to these old truths from time to time. To the extent that the things taught by these Westminster divines are scriptural, then we must return to these, repaint them from time to time, and hold fast. We might do this better as a covenantal family, rather than as individuals. It's time to look through the windows and then grab a bucket of white paint to repair the ancient landmarks. Thomas Smyth returns us to the family motif, as he assessed the value of proper commemorations at the bicentennial: "Like the members of a large family we have been scattered, and lived apart, and gathered around us new and separate interests. But we are on this occasion brought together. We revisit our old ancestral home-stead. We read over the original deeds by which we became heirs to the same rich inheritance. The ties of blood draw our hearts together, and we embrace one another in the arms of spiritual affection."[22]

At every family commemoration, let us adopt the resolve and imperative of the Psalmist: "I will remember the deeds of the Lord; yes, I will remember your miracles of long ago. I will meditate on all your works and consider all your mighty deeds" (Ps. 77:11, 12).

Questions for Review.

1. Can you summarize some of the motivations and highlights of earlier commemorations?

183

2. Review some of the Psalms which teach the value of remembering. Why do you think that these contain such an emphasis?

3. Read Hebrews 11:4–12:3. How can this passage guide a commemoration?

4. What happens when people do not remember the works of the Lord? Can you give an illustration from modern history of this?

5. What needs to be done in local churches to insure that biblical truth continues in our churches? What can you do to help in this area?

For Discussion.

1. How have attitudes toward our past history shifted in the twentieth century? Is this good?

2. How are these commemorations similar to family reunions?

3. After this study, how are you better prepared to (a) appreciate your church's past, and (b) guard against idolatry?

Spotlight: Stephen Marshall

Stephen Marshall, born in Huntingdonshire, England and educated at Emmanuel College, was one of the finest preachers and leaders in mid- seventeenth century England. He was known as a "reaper in God's Harvest" and Richard Baxter spoke of him as a "sober and worthy man." Marshall served as a minister at Finchingfield and was frequently called on to preach to the Long Parliament.

One biographer estimated his influence as a leader of the Assembly: "No man was more gracious....He was their trumpet, by whom they sounded their solemn Fasts, preaching more public sermons on that occasion, than any four of his [colleagues]. In their sickness he was their confessor, in their assembly their counselor, in their treaties their chaplain, in their disputations their champion.' Clarendon says, 'And without doubt, the Archbishop of Canterbury had never so great an influence upon the councils at court, as Mr. Marshall and Dr. Burgess had upon the Houses of Parliament.' " On one solemn Fasting Day before the House of Commons in 1640 it is reported that Dr. Burgess and Mr. Marshall preached at least seven hours, so intent were they to communicate the message of the cross.

In 1641, a pamphlet was published, in which defenders of the divine right of Presbyterianism debated the Anglican church's claim to priority. A written response to Bishop Hall's *Humble Remonstrance* (a work defending the episcopal form of government), was issued under the odd name of Smectymnuus. Later it was discovered that this was an acronym, composed of letters from the names of five leading Presbyterian co-authors in London: Stephen Marshall, Edmund Calamy, Thomas Young, Matthew Newcomen and William Spurstow. Stephen Marshall was not only a great expositor, but an ecclesiastical churchman of mighty thought and conviction as well. Marshall was also one of the first to argue for the institution of ruling elders by divine mandate.

Later he served as a chaplain to the Earl of Essex. Shortly after the Westminster Assembly convened, Stephen Marshall and Philip Nye were sent to accompany the Scottish commissioners back to Edinburgh, there to negotiate a treaty.

After the Scots adopted the resulting Solemn League and Covenant, Marshall co-wrote a letter which concluded with these sentiments: "We scarcely ever saw so much of Christ for us as this day, in the Assembly's carrying of this business, such weeping, such rejoicing, such resolution, such pathetical expressions, as we confess hath much refreshed our hearts, before extremely saddened with ill news from our dear country; and hath put us in good hope that this nation, which sets about this business, as becometh the work of God and saving of the kingdoms, shall be the means of lifting up distressed England and Ireland."

Marshall has been given various epitaphs which convey his colorful personality, variously having been called, "the great bell-weather of Presbyterians," "a famous incendiary, and assistant to the Parliamentarians," "the Geneva-Bull, and a factious and rebellious divine," "and the Archflamen of the rebellious rout." It has been said, "that he left behind him few laborers like himself; that he was a Christian in practice as well as in profession; that he lived by faith, and died by faith, and was an example to the believers, in word, in conversation, in charity, in faith, and in purity....Respecting his death, he said, 'I cannot say, as one did, I have not so lived that I should now be afraid to die; but this I can say, I have so learned Christ, that I am not afraid to die.' " Marshall died in November, 1655, and left behind a number of printed sermons and the longer 1666 *A Defense of Infant-Baptism* which was dedicated to the Assembly of divines and commissioners of the Church of Scotland then sitting at Westminster.

Appendix: Want to Know More?

A revival of interest in orthodox Reformed belief has led to a republishing of Westminster era and other Puritan works. Several smaller publishers are to be thanked for this: The Banner of Truth Trust, Still Waters Revival Books, Soli Deo Gloria Publications, Presbyterian Heritage Publications, Naphtali Press and Sprinkle Publications.

Some of the more accessible writings are divided here into four categories: (1) primary resources, recently reprinted; (2) histories of the Westminster Assembly; (3) commentaries and commemoratives; and (4) recent writings.

Primary Resources, recently reprinted

The Works of George Gillespie (2 vols.) is available from Still Waters Revival Books, Edmonton, Canada. See especially "Notes of Debates and Proceedings of the Assembly of Divines at Westminster, February 1644 to January 1645" in vol. 2.

Two other primary sources by Still Waters Revival Books are *The Minutes of the Sessions of the Westminster Assembly of Divines* (A. F. Mitchell and John Struthers, eds.), 1874 (Reprint, 1992) and Samuel Rutherford's *Due Right of Presbyteries* 1644 (Reprint 1993). Both provide glimpses into the governmental debates of the Assembly.

These primary sources are more difficult reading than the secondary materials. The beginner might want to come back to these after mastering some of the other materials. For more insight into the piety of some of the other contemporaries at the Westminster Assembly, several publishers provide reprints of various authors' works. More than a few Christians have ventured out, like gold miners, and struck Puritan gold.

Soli Deo Gloria Publications specializes in reprinting the works of seventeenth century Puritans. They have offered the *Practical Works of Richard Baxter* (4 vols.), who, while not appointed to the Assembly held much in common with participants. Either *The Works of William Bridge* (5 vols.) or Obadiah Sedgwick's *The Anatomy of Secret Sins* would be useful and rewarding.

Banner of Truth also offers works by Westminster divines: *Lifting Up for the Downcast* by William Bridge, *Rare Jewel of Christian Contentment* by Jeremiah Burroughs and *The Reformed Pastor* by Richard Baxter.

Several individual volumes by Jeremiah Burroughs are available from Soli Deo Gloria: *The Evil of Evils, The Saint's Happiness* (on the Beatitudes), *A Treatise of Earthly-Mindedness, Gospel Fear, Gospel Worship* (a fine statement of the regulative principle), and *The Saints' Treasury*, a collection of five sermons, e.g., "Christ is all in all," and "The Glorious Enjoyment of Heavenly Things by Faith."

Also available from Soli Deo Gloria are Edward Reynolds' *The Sinfulness of Sin, The Select Works of Thomas Case* and a collection of *Farewell Sermons* preached by many of the divines at the 1662 Great Ejection.

Histories of the Westminster Assembly

William Beveridge's *A Short History of the Westminster Assembly*, originally printed in Edinburgh in 1904 (reprinted in 1991 by A Press), includes a history of the Puritan separation and a chapter on the calling/convocation of the Assembly. It also has discussions of background, including the Solemn League and Covenant, and a scope of the Assembly's deliberations and works, with special chapters on church government, the Confession of Faith and the Catechisms. This is a great beginning place, if one has never read anything about the Assembly. It is non-technical and makes good use of the primary sources.

Near the bicentennial of the Westminster Assembly, it became apparent that there was no standard history of that monumental Synod. Although several of the actual participants (Baillie, Gillespie, Goodwin, Lightfoot) took notes, most were either not widely available, or lost by the time of this bicentennial. When he wrote his *History of the Westminster Assembly of Divines* in 1843 (reprinted by Still Waters Revival Books in 1993), William Hetherington thought the minutes of the Assembly had been hopelessly lost. Hence prior to Alexander F. Mitchell's 1874 printing of the minutes, Hetherington's work was definitive, although incomplete. As a historical writing, it is still an excellent history for the reading public.

Another important history of the Westminster Assembly was *A History of the Westminster Assembly Divines, Embracing an Account of its Principal Transactions and Biographical Sketches,* authored in 1841 by A. W. Mitchell (not related to A. F. Mitchell). This history, too, reviews the background leading up to the Assembly and includes a collection of biographical sketches of the Assembly Divines.

Alexander F. Mitchell's *The Westminster Assembly: Its History and Standards* was reprinted by Still Waters Revival Books in 1993. This classic, written by one of the greatest students of the Westminster Assembly, ranks as one of the finest histories.

Another excellent treatise on the Assembly is Benjamin B. Warfield's *The Westminster Assembly and Its Work*, 1931 (also in *The Complete Works of Benjamin Warfield* [Baker, 1980]), and reprinted by Still Waters Revival Books in 1991. The chapters on the work of the Assembly, and the Westminster Confession provide the most historical detail.

The Banner of Truth Trust reprinted in 1982 the bulk of James Reid's 1811 *The Memoirs of the Westminster Assembly Divines*. In this volume Reid puts together inspirational biographical sketches and accounts of the divines. The "Spotlight" biographies drew heavily on this work and we thank Banner of Truth for granting premission to use this material.

One of the most thorough histories of the Westminster Assembly is *Minutes of the Sessions of the Westminster Assembly of Divines* (Mitchell and Struthers, eds.). This 1874 book was reprinted in 1992 by Still Waters Revival Books and provides an excellent view of the Assembly sessions. While not a complete listing of the minutes, this is a helpful guide to many for the true sentiments and original intents of the Assembly.

Commentaries and Commemorations

The tradition of commenting on the Westminster Standards is a long and respected one. See, for example, James Fisher's *The Assembly's Shorter Catechism Explained* (1753 with Ebenezer and Ralph Erskine, then reprinted in 1843), S. D. Salmon's *An Exposition of the Shorter Catechism* (1800), and Matthew Henry's *An Exposition of the Shorter Catechism* (1850). Additional commentaries on the standards are A. A. Hodge's (1869) and Robert Shaw's *The Reformed Faith: An Exposition of the Westminster Confession of Faith* (available from Christian Focus Publications). Banner of Truth also offers the short, but worthwhile *Shorter Catechism Explained* by Thomas Vincent, taken from the 1674 edition endorsed by Puritan exemplars, Owen, Watson, Manton, Calamy and Brooks. John Whitecross's *Anecdotes Illustrative of the Assembly* was reprinted by Banner of Truth in 1968 as *The Shorter Catechism Illustrated*.

The Southern Presbyterian Church in its 1897 *Memorial Volume of the Westminster Assembly, 1647–1897* and the Northern Presbyterian Church in *Anniversary Addresses* (1898) commemorated the Assembly with fine collections of essays. In addition, Banner of Truth published the addresses from the 350th anniversary in London.

In 1943 John Murray wrote a number of articles on the Westminster Assembly. Among them were "A Notable Tercentenary" (see *The Collected Works of John Murray*, vol. 1, chapter 42 [Banner of Truth, 1980]); "The Importance and Relevance of the Westminster Confession" (vol. 4); "The Theology of the Westminster Confession of Faith" (vol. 4); and a number of reviews of works on the Assembly authored in the twentieth century. Murray was helpful in reviewing Samuel Carruthers's *The Everyday Work of the Westminster Assembly*, 1943.

Recent Publications

The tradition of commenting on the Westminster Standards is alive and well in our own time. A recent work, which combines simplicity of presentation and insight, is *A Guide to the Westminster Confession*, a commentary by John H. Gerstner, Douglas F. Kelly and Philip Rollinson. This volume which may be used by elders, for training groups, and Sunday School Classes, as well as for personal reference, is available from Summertown Texts. John Gerstner's *Themes from the Westminster Confession of Faith* (1991) is an introductory study of the themes of the Confession. Two other helpful treatments are G. I. Williamson's *The Westminster Confession of Faith for Study Classes* (Presbyterian and Reformed, 1985) and Morton Smith's *Harmony of the Westminster Confession and Catechisms*, a commentary on the standards (Greenville Presbyterian Theological Seminary Press). On a popular level, *How to Teach the Catechism to Children* (1979) by Mrs. Frank Horton and *Studies in the Shorter Catechism* by Paul Settle are helpful tools.

In 1993 Still Waters Revival Books republished a two-volume commentary by Thomas Ridgely on the Westminster Larger Catechism. One of the most extensive commentaries has been Thomas Boston's *Commentary on the Shorter Catechism* (over 1300 pp. in 2 vol., available from Still Waters Revival Books). One might also consult *A Guide to the Westminster Confession of Faith* by James Bordwine (Greenville Theological Seminary Press). One could also profit from Gordon Clark's *What Presbyterians Believe* (1963), a short study course on the Confession of Faith (Presbyterian and Reformed). A recent edition of the Confession of Faith, "A Contemporary Edition," which is faithful to the original, has been compiled by Donald Remillard (Presby Press).

In April 1993, the *Presbyterian Reformed Magazine* printed a special Westminster Assembly Commemorative edition, re-printing the following: by John Murray, as earlier published in *The Presbyterian Guardian*—"The Westminster Standards," "The Calling of the Westminster Assembly," "The Work of the Westminster Assembly," "The Catechisms of the Westminster Assembly," and "The Fourth Commandment According to the Westminster Standards"; excerpts from Fisher's 1753 Catechism; extracts from Thornwell and Dabney; William Symington's "Historical Sketch of the Westminster Assembly of Divines" (1843), and an article on William Twisse by William Young.

Finally, computer-related resources are increasingly available. The first of these was Raymond Dillard's 1988 *Concordance to the Westminster Standards* (also, the Confession and Catechisms are on disk). Since then Westminster Media has released these on share-ware that is inexpensive and accessible. At present, Mr. Michael Bushell (c/o 11604 Stewart Lane, Silver Spring, MD) is developing a computer program interfacing the Westminster Standards and Scripture references.

Often, the average Christian is intimidated by these materials, assuming that they are too complex. However, these are some of the most straightforward and uncomplicated writings in Reformed history. One does not need to be a seminary graduate to benefit from these resources.

One reason to study some of these books is their devotional value. As Reg Barrows says of the recently released Boston *Commentary on the Shorter Catechism:* "Its pages breathe with the...singlehearted devotion to Christ and His jealousies for truth, in that special way that only these old Puritan writings can! It matters not where you open this work...it draws you in and engulfs your soul with edification; opening the treasures of our Lord's wisdom while eliciting praises of thankfulness; but, on the other hand never shrinking back from declaring the whole counsel of God."

Publishers and sources listed alphabetically:

A Press in Greenville, South Carolina, P.O. Box 8796, Greenville, S.C. 29604

Banner of Truth Trust, Box 621, Carlisle, PA 17013

Christian Focus Publications, Geanies House, Fearn, Tain, Ross-shire IV20 1TW, Scotland

Greenville Theological Seminary Press, P.O. Box 9279, Greenville, SC 29604

Presby Press, 37371 Clubhouse Drive, Sterling Heights, MI 48312

Presbyterian Reformed Magazine, 2408 Holt Street, Vienna, VA 22180

Soli Deo Gloria Publications, 213 W. Vincent, Ligonier, PA 15658–1139

Still Waters Revival Books, 4710 37A Ave., Edmonton, AB, Canada T6L 3T5

Summertown Texts, P. O. Box 453, Signal Mountain, TN 37377

Westminster Media, P.O. Box 27009, Philadelphia, PA 19118

Notes

Introduction—Remembering
1. Lord Acton, cited in John Briggs, "God, Time and History," in *Eerdmans' Handbook to the History of Christianity*, ed. Tim Dowley (Grand Rapids: Wm. B. Eerdmans Publishing Co., 1977), p. 2.
2. George Grant, *Third Time Around* (Nashville: Wolgemuth and Hyatt, 1991), p. 180.
3. William Henry Roberts, ed., *Addresses at the Celebration of the Two-Hundred and Fiftieth Anniversary of the Westminster Assembly* (Philadelphia: Presbyterian Board of Publication, 1898) p. 273 (hereafter cited as *Anniversary Addresses* [1898]).

Chapter 1. Origins of the Assembly
1. Briggs, "God, Time and History," p. 2.
2. A. W. Mitchell, *A History of the Westminster Assembly of Divines* (Philadelphia: Presbyterian Board of Publication, 1841), p. 2.
3. Ibid., pp. 18–19.
4. *Journal of Presbyterian History* 21, nos. 2, 3, pp. 126–127.
5. A. W. Mitchell [1841], p. 29.
6. Ibid., p. 33.
7. William M. Hetherington, *History of the Westminster Assembly of Divines* (1856; reprint ed., Edmonton, AB: Still Waters Revival Books, 1993), p. 125.
8. A. W. Mitchell [1841], p. 36.

Chapter 2. Parties, Procedures and Politics
1. A. W. Mitchell [1841], p. 169.
2. William Beveridge, *A Short History of the Westminster Assembly* (1904; reprint ed., South Carolina: A Press, 1991) p. 92.
3. James Reid, *The Memoirs of the Westminster Divines* (1811; reprint ed., 2 vols., Edinburgh: Banner of Truth Trust, 1982) 1: 240.
4. A. W. Mitchell [1841], p. 49.
5. Beveridge, p. 63.
6. A. W. Mitchell [1841], p. 52.
7. *Anniversary Addresses* (1898), p. 136.

8. A. W. Mitchell [1841], p. 30–31.
9. J. McDowell Richards in *Union Seminary Review* 54, no. 1 (1943): 333.
10. Ibid., p. 113.
11. Beveridge, p. 60.
12. Richards, *Union Seminary Review* 54, no. 1 (1943): 333.
13. Francis Patton, *The Genesis of the Westminster Assembly* (Richmond, VA: Presbyterian Committee of Publication, 1889) pp. 79–80.
14. Walter L. Lingle, "The Story of the Westminster Assembly," *Union Seminary Review* 54, no. 1 (1943): 327.
15. Ibid., p. 326.
16. A. W. Mitchell [1841], p. 120.

Chapter 3. The Players

1. Francis R. Beattie et al., *Memorial Volume of the Westminster Assembly, 1647–1897* (Richmond: The Presbyterian Committee of Publication, 1897), p. 4 (hereafter cited as *Memorial Volume*).
2. Beveridge, p. 26.
3. Ibid., p. 24.
4. A. W. Mitchell [1841], p. 31.
5. *Memorial Volume*, p. 68.
6. Ibid.
7. Hetherington, p. 400.
8. Ibid., p. 402.
9. *Anniversary Addresses* (1898), p. 138.
10. Beveridge, p. 29.
11. Hetherington, p. 400.
12. Alexander F. Mitchell, *The Westminster Assembly: Its History and Standards* (Edmonton, AB: Still Waters Revival Books, 1992), pp. 314-316.
13. *Memorial Volume*, p. 76.
14. *Anniversary Addresses* (1898), pp. 53–54.
15. Ibid.
16. Ibid.
17. Ibid., p. 43.
18. Ibid., p. 55.

Chapter 4. God's Scriptures

1. Anthony Burgess, cited in Benjamin B. Warfield's, *The Westminster Assembly and Its Work* (1931; reprint ed., Edmonton, AB: Still Waters Revival Books, 1991) p. 208.

2. Ibid., p. 155.
3. Ibid.
4. Ibid., p. 176.
5. Ibid., p. 197.
6. Ibid., p. 199.
7. Ibid., p. 333.
8. Ibid., p. 221.
9. Ibid., p. 256.
10. Ibid.
11. Ibid.
12. Ibid., pp. 256–257.

Chapter 5. God's Sovereignty

1. *Anniversary Addresses* (1898), p. 132.
2. *Memorial Volume*, p. 63.
3. John Murray, *The Collected Works of John Murray*, vol. 1 (Pennsylvania: The Banner of Truth Trust, 1980), p. 212.
4. Warfield, p. 123.
5. Ibid.
6. Ibid., pp. 146–147.
7. *Anniversary Addresses* (1898), p. 133.

Chapter 6. God's Salvation

1. Dorothy L. Sayers, *The Whimsical Christian* (New York: Macmillan Publishing Company, 1978)

Chapter 7. God's Society

1. *Anniversary Addresses* (1898), p. 133.
2. Warfield, p. 123.
3. Thomas Smyth, "History of the Westminster Assembly," in *The Works of Thomas Smyth* (Columbia, SC: Bryan Publishing, 1908) p. 398.
4. Walter Travers, *The Book of Discipline* in David Hall and Joseph Hall, *Paradigms in Polity* (Grand Rapids: Wm. B. Eerdmans Publishing Co., 1994–).
5. Baillie, *Dissuasive From the Errors of the Time* 1646, cited in Thomas M'Crie, *Unity of the Church* (Dallas: Presbyterian Heritage Publications, 1989) pp. 187–188.
6. Hetherington, pp. 160–161.
7. A. F. Mitchell, pp. 267–268.

Chapter 8. Influence of the Westminster Assembly
1. Lingle, *Union Seminary Review* 54, no. 1 (1943): 321.
2. A. W. Mitchell [1841], p. 169.
3. Beveridge, p. 3.
4. *Memorial Volume*, p. 198.
5. William G. T. Shedd, *Calvinism: Pure and Mixed* (Edinburgh: Banner of Truth, 1986) p. 161.
6. Ibid., p. xvii.
7. Ibid., p. xviii.
8. Ibid.
9. *Anniversary Addresses* (1898), pp. 126–127.
10. Ibid., p. 131.
11. Ibid., p. 144.
12. C. K. Chesterton, *Orthodoxy* (New York: Doubleday, 1990), p. 74.
13. *Anniversary Addresses* (1898), p. 145.
14. Ibid., p. 176.
15. Ibid., p. 188.
16. Beveridge, p. 140.
17. *Memorial Volume*, pp. 136–137.
18. *Union Seminary Review* 54, no. 1 (1943): 341.
19. *Anniversary Addresses* (1898), p. 77.
20. Hetherington, p. 156.
21. A. W. Mitchell [1841], pp. 178–179.
22. Murray, 1:312.

Chapter 9. The Spirituality of the Assembly
1. *Memorial Volume*, pp. 261–262.
2. Reid, 1: 130.
3. A. W. Mitchell [1841], pp. 169.
4. Ibid., p. 38.
5. Beveridge, p. 32.
6. A. F. Mitchell, p. 139.
7. Reid, 1: 380.
8. Ibid.
9. Beveridge, pp. 81–82.
10. A. W. Mitchell [1841], pp. 54, 56, 58.
11. Reid, 1: 182–183.
12. Ibid., 2: 101.
13. Ibid., 2: 21.
14. Ibid., 2: 23.
15. Ibid.
16. Ibid.

17. Samuel Carruthers, *The Everyday Work of the Westminster Assembly* (London: Presbyterian Historical Society, 1943), p. 70.
18. Reid, 2: 6.
19. Carruthers, p. 76.
20. *Memorial Volume*, pp. 257–258, 260.
21. Ibid., p. 263.
22. Helen C. White, Ruth C. Wallerstein and Ticardo Quintana, eds., *Seventeenth Century Verse and Prose*, Vol. 1 (New York: Macmillan, 1951), p. 265.
23. *Memorial Volume*, pp. 268–269.
24. Reid, 2: 232–234.
25. *Memorial Volume*, pp. 263–264.
26. Reid, 2: 3.

Chapter 10. Critics of the Assembly

1. Sydney Ahlstrom, *A Religious History of the American People,* vol. 1 (New York: Doubleday, 1975), p. 136.
2. *Journal of Presbyterian History* 21, nos. 2, 3, pp. 122–123.
3. A. F. Mitchell, pp. 129–130.
4. *Journal of Presbyterian History* 21, nos. 2, 3, pp. 120–121.
5. Beveridge, p. 20.
6. A. W. Mitchell [1841], pp. 175–176.
7. Ibid., pp. 168–169.
8. Beveridge, p. 23.
9. *Journal of Presbyterian History* 21, nos. 2, 3, pp. 140.
10. Beveridge, p. 86.
11. A. W. Mitchell [1841], pp. 173–174.
12. *Memorial Volume*, p. 81.
13. Ibid.
14. *Journal of Presbyterian History* 21, nos. 2, 3, p. 160.
15. Ibid., p. 161.
16. Ibid.
17. Ibid., p. 137.
18. Ibid., p. 138.
19. Ibid., p. 139.
20. Ibid., p. 141.
21. Ibid., p. 142.
22. Ibid., p. 145.
23. Ibid., p. 146.
24. Ibid., p. 147.
25. Ibid.
26. Beveridge, p. 83.

27. C. S. Lewis, *The Abolition of Man* (New York: Macmillan, 1947), p. 60.

Chapter 11. Why Remember?

1. *Anniversary Addresses* (1898), p. 274.
2. William Symington, "Historical Sketch of the Westminster Assembly of Divines" in *Commemoration of the Bicentenary of the Westminster Divines* (Glasgow, 1843) pp. 69, 71.
3. Smyth, p. 393.
4. Ibid., p. 191.
5. Hetherington, pp. 349–351.
6. *Anniversary Addresses* (1898), p. 273.
7. Shedd, p. 159.
8. Ibid., p. 160.
9. *Memorial Volume*, pp. xvi–xvii.
10. Ibid., p. 189.
11. *Journal of Presbyterian History* 21, nos. 2, 3, p. 102.
12. Fredrick Jones in *Stewardship Journal*, Fall 1992, vol. 2, no. 3, p. 62.
13. George Grant and Mark Horne, *Unnatural Affections* (Franklin, TN: Legacy, 1992), p. 44.
14. *Memorial Volume*, p. 254.
15. Symington, pp. 31–32.
16. Cited in Grant's, *Third Time Around*, p. 159.
17. Cited in Rush Limbaugh's, *The Way Things Ought to Be* (New York: Simon and Schuster, 1992)
18. Milan Hubl, cited in Grant's, *Third Time Around*, p. 136.
19. London: SCM Press, 1991, p. 1.
20. *The Romance of Faith* (New York: Doubleday, 1980), pp. 114–115.
21. Frederick W. Loetscher, "Early American Presbyterianism" in *Journal of Presbyterian History*, Dec. 1929, vol. 8, no. 8, p. 23.
22. Smyth, p. 428.

Selected Bibliography

Beattie, Francis R. et al. *Memorial Volume of the Westminster Assembly, 1647–1897.* Richmond: The Presbyterian Committee of Publication, 1897.

Beveridge, William. *A Short History of the Westminster Assembly.* 1904. Reprint. South Carolina: A Press, 1991.

Carruthers, Samuel. *The Everyday Work of the Westminster Assembly.* London: Presbyterian Historical Society, 1943.

Gillespie, George. *The Works of George Gillespie.* Edmonton, AB: Still Waters Revival Books, 1991. Vol. 2.

Hall, Peter, ed. *The Harmony of Protestant Confessions.* Edmonton, AB: Still Waters Revival Books, 1992.

Hetherington, William M. *History of the Westminster Assembly of Divines.* 1856. Reprint. Edmonton, AB: Still Waters Revival Books, 1993.

Holley, Larry. *The Divines of the Westminster Assembly: A Study of Puritanism and Parliament.* New Haven: Yale University Press, 1979.

Mitchell, Alexander F. *The Westminster Assembly: Its History and Standards.* Edmonton, AB: Still Waters Revival Books, 1992.

Mitchell, Alexander F. and Struthers, John, eds. *Minutes of the Sessions of the Westminster Assembly of Divines.* 1874. Reprint. Edmonton, AB: Still Waters Revival Books, 1992.

Mitchell, A. W. *A History of the Westminster Assembly of Divines.* Philadelphia: Presbyterian Board of Publication, 1841.

Paul, Robert F. *The Assembly of the Lord.* Edinburgh: T and T Clark, 1985.

Reid, James. *The Memoirs of the Westminster Divines.* 1811. Reprint. 2 vols. Edinburgh: Banner of Truth Trust, 1982.

Roberts, William Henry, ed. *Addresses at the Celebration of the Two-Hundred and Fiftieth Anniversary of the Westminster Assembly.* Philadelphia: Presbyterian Board of Publication, 1898.

Shedd, William G. T. *Calvinism: Pure and Mixed.* Edinburgh: Banner of Truth, 1986.

Smyth, Thomas. "History of the Westminster Assembly." In *The Works of Thomas Smyth.* Columbia, SC: Bryan Publishing, 1908.

Symington, William. "Historical Sketch of the Westminster Assembly of Divines." In *Commemoration of the Bicentenary of the Westminster Divines.* Glasgow, 1843.

Warfield, Benjamin B. *The Westminster Assembly and Its Work.* 1932. Reprint. Edmonton, AB: Still Waters Revival Books, 1991.